Coosa County
Turkey Tales

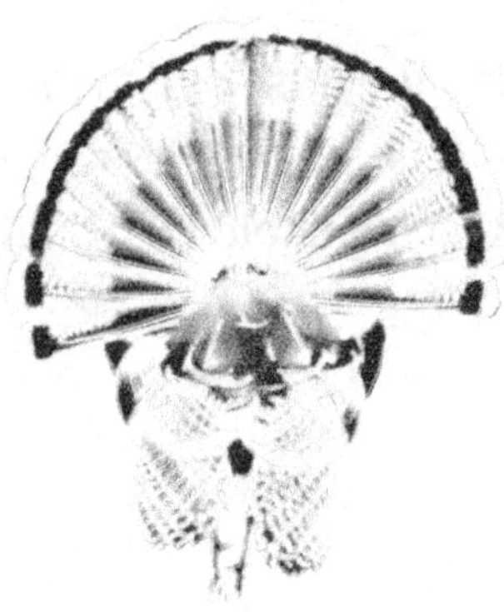

Joel D. Glover

Dedication

Anyone who knew me probably knew I loved to hunt wild turkeys. I was so blessed by the Lord to land in Coosa County with its tremendous turkey population. I was so tremendously blessed to find folks who would teach me to hunt and to develop friendships with some folks who would let me hunt on their property. That was something I never took for granted and did not assume would be made available to me each season. It was something much too valuable for me to take for granted. I dedicate this book to my dear friends and brother and sister in Christ, Randy and Susan. I love you and I can't thank you enough for sharing your Treasure with me. Thank you for loving me and my family!

Disclaimer

The stories in this book are true to the best of my knowledge and recollection. I changed many of the names. I'm certain you will find some of these stories difficult to believe. As I've said before, I found them hard to believe and I was there! These are my stories for your enjoyment. If you think you recognize someone in here, it's probably just your imagination.

Contents

It's a Fickle Bird

DO YOU EVER FORGET the first gobbler you called in and gave a ride in your truck? I hope not. I sure remember my first one. After being hired as a wildlife biologist with Alabama Game and Fish and getting settled in Coosa County, I invited my dear friend from graduate school, Phillip Blake to come and pursue the elusive monarch of the woods. I remember the hunt and in my mind's eye I can still see the bird coming in. Although I felt he might be a little far for my two-and-three-quarter-inch gun, I shot the gobbler at thirty-eight steps. I rushed over to the flopping bird and claimed my prize. The bird sported a nine-and-a-half-inch beard and didn't have a spur on either leg. Although I felt just a little cheated, he was my trophy and I was very proud of him.

During my tutelage in turkey hunting one of the things that Phil told me several times was that the wild turkey is a fickle bird. I must admit I wasn't exactly sure what that meant way back then; however, after over thirty years of gobbler chasing, I definitely understand it now.

If you look up the word *fickle* in the dictionary it is defined as "marked by lack of steadfastness, constancy, or stability: given to erratic changeableness." Man, have I experienced erratic changeableness! Let me explain. Many times, I have lamented about a gobbler's lack of consistency. The past season was no exception.

Late in the season, Phil called and asked if we could get together and try our luck with the turkeys. I told him we would definitely make that happen. I had hunted my uncle's small tract a couple of days earlier and had heard a couple of birds. A couple of days later, Phil and I were standing on the property listening for gobbles. A gobbler responded to a crow and I told Phil I knew the exact tree where he was roosted. We were soon set up about sixty-five yards from the gobbling bird. Phil was sitting about twenty-five feet in front of me and toward the bird. I called sparingly and the bird answered everything I did.

Some of the calls were so quiet I wasn't sure Phil could hear them; however, the gobbler did and responded with lusty gobbles. Finally, after about forty-five minutes of gobbling in the tree, we saw the bird fly down. With him on the ground, I offered a few yelps and I immediately heard the bird drumming. I got my gun to my shoulder and waited for the bird to appear. We both kept scanning for the gobbler we knew would soon come into view. We kept scanning and waiting. And waiting. I eventually gave another call that was immediately followed by silence. After a few minutes I crawled over to Phil and asked him what had happened. He replied he had seen the bird fly down and that was it.

I tried some loud calling that I hoped would get the bird to sound off. Evidently the bird's shift had ended as we did not hear another turkey sound.

As we gathered our gear and started walking out, I looked at my gobble counter and saw I had recorded sixty-five gobbles. We discussed what had taken place and really couldn't come up with anything we should have done differently. Although we were a little disappointed that the bird did not come in, we agreed it was a great hunt nonetheless.

The next day, my son and I decided to give the bird another try. When he gobbled in pretty much the same spot, I decided we would set up south of him, which was the opposite from where Phil and I had tried. The bird flew down rather quickly and I began calling. While he answered rather aggressively, he walked directly to where Phil and I had been set up. After gobbling twenty-eight times, he walked away.

Two days later I was once again on the property. This time the bird had moved about two hundred yards to the east which put him on the neighboring property. I went toward him and sat up about fifty yards from the property line. The bird answered me regularly but also answered two other hens I could hear. I moved up and down the line but nothing seemed to sway the old boy. I decided to head back toward the truck. As I got to the top of the hill, I gave another call, which was answered by what I felt was a second gobbler to the north. Unfortunately, he was also off the property and across a large creek.

I walked another fifty yards and yelped again and received another gobble. I was now standing within forty yards of where Phil and I had been days earlier, so I slid into the familiar spot and started calling. I could tell the bird was moving toward me at a slow pace. Soon I realized there were now two gobbling birds. Eventually I wasn't sure whether there were two or three gobblers. Although the birds never got closer than about 150 yards, I had a ringside seat at Gobblefest. The birds were gobbling at me and each other and it continued for a while. Finally, the gobbling subsided and I decided it was over. I looked at my gobble counter and was amazed to see it read 318 gobbles! What a tremendous day. I couldn't wait for the next morning.

As is usual during the turkey season, I was awake well before the alarm was set to come on. I got dressed and headed for the woods. I picked up Hogan, the fourteen-year-old who had been hunting with me on nonschool days, and shared with him the events of the previous day. He could not believe the birds had gobbled so many times. This was his first year turkey hunting. We had been fortunate enough to call in and kill a gobbler on his first ever hunt, so of course he was hooked.

We made it to the property and headed up on the hill where I had been the day before. As usual I thoroughly enjoyed hearing the woods come to life. Everything was sounding off, including two close-by barred owls that were talking it up. The only thing that wasn't saying a word was, you guessed it, the gobblers. Owl hoots, crow caws, and a pileated woodpecker were all unsuccessful in soliciting a single gobble.

As we were headed back toward the truck, Hogan asked me what I thought had happened. I told him that a turkey was a fickle bird, given to erratic changeableness, and you never could count on what happened today happening tomorrow. He did not miss a beat and replied, "I guess that's why they call them turkeys." I couldn't argue with that.

Speaking the Language

DEDICATED TURKEY HUNTERS are a different breed. Rising well before dawn is a small price to pay to get to witness the world coming to life. If a turkey gobbler decides to split that morning calm with a lusty gobble, it makes it better. If he doesn't come to that decision on his own, we will do our best to get him to contribute a gobble or better yet a whole bunch of gobbles. If you spend a lot of time in the turkey woods, you will hear and see things and likely do things that people won't believe. Most turkey hunters keep those things to themselves unless they are sharing them with the like-minded. Many years ago, as I contemplated our actions, thoughts, and jargon, I realized why we keep a lot of it to ourselves. It's because others wouldn't understand it or believe it if we were to tell them. Thinking about that, I wrote the following story. I hope you can relate to and enjoy it.

I hadn't intended to eavesdrop, but what these guys were saying amazed and astounded me. The turkey hunters were so excited I could not help but overhear their conversation in a local restaurant. Now I'm not opposed to hunting and have done some of it myself. I've also been known to tell a story or two and maybe even stretch a fish or add a point to a buck's rack. But none of my experiences had prepared me for what I was about to hear. I had thought about giving turkey hunting a try but I really didn't know much about it. I had heard that wild turkeys were different than their tame relatives. Listening to these guys had me wondering if I even wanted to see one. I swear they were speaking a different language.

I knew these guys probably weren't the sharpest knives in the drawer when I heard them say they had been standing in the woods at daylight hooting like an owl. I had an uncle that used to do that; of course, that was how we were able to find him after he had gotten into the special cough medicine that was kept in the back room!

I wasn't sure these guys were even talking about turkey hunting until one of them said he heard a turkey and went to set up on it. I must admit this sounded weird. Why would someone want to sit on a turkey? That was beyond me. Evidently the turkey didn't like it much either. I think it must have bitten the guy since he said he yelped a few times. I thought, Well, it's good enough for you.

The more I listened, the more confused I got. I was having trouble following the story. I guess I should say they were just bird hunting because they weren't only after turkeys. I heard one say he used a crow call, hawk call, and woodpecker call, while another one was using a peacock call. When they asked another guy how he had done, he replied that he had heard a turkey and it was hammering. This conjured up an interesting picture in my mind. He said the turkey was hammering at everything. Then he said he could see the bird coming through the woods and it had a long beard that he wanted to add to his collection! At this point, I felt confident that he was aware I was listening and was just having some fun with me. Either that or I was in a bad episode of *The Twilight Zone*! The hunter continued and said he was sure the bird would have a good set of hooks. I must admit I was at a total loss about why a turkey would have hooks! Even more puzzling was why was this guy pursuing a turkey that was obviously someone's pet, and why did he want to shave its beard off and keep it? I'll admit I have a nice set of antlers on my wall at home, but I didn't shave any of the hair off and keep it! I've heard of people tanning hides and stuff but this sounded very different.

Just when I thought things were bad, it got even worse. He said he began to cut at the turkey. I had thought people hunted turkeys with shotguns! I wondered what kind of sicko would try to cut a turkey. Even worse was the fact I could tell this guy was getting more and more excited as he told his sick story. Then he said he heard a hen and she was whining. I thought, I guess so, you'd whine too if somebody was stabbing one of your family members.

I thought he might have in fact cut himself because he said he began yelping. He then said he thought the turkey had hung up. I thought I would have hung up on this guy a long time ago. The man said the bird began spitting and drumming. I was once again confused. I guess the bird was probably mad enough to spit, but I didn't get the drum part. Evidently the drumming really irritated the guy because he said the hair on his neck stood up and he started throwing his calls. This was making very little sense to me.

It must have been getting warm because he said he saw that the turkey had a fan. He said when he saw that he got really excited and started cutting at the turkey again.

I realized the situation was beginning to deteriorate when he told the others he decided he would have to belly crawl up on the turkey. I really didn't want to hear what would happen next, but I was in too deep to stop now. Undoubtedly, the hunter must have crawled through some poison ivy because he told the others that he began aggressively scratching. However, I was once again confused when he said he was scratching in the leaves. I then realized he might be looking for the calls he had said he was throwing earlier.

Apparently, these guys used several different methods to catch the poor turkeys. I heard him say he didn't want to flush the bird, which conjured up some odd images in my mind. Then I was totally confused when he said he wasn't sure whether to use a box or a tube. One of the guys chimed in that he would have used a diaphragm, which confused me even more. Another one said he thought it was best to use a glass! I had to assume that was what they kept cutting at the bird with!

Just as I thought it couldn't get much more confusing, he said he thought the gobbler was close enough to reach with his three-and-a-half-inch gun. I thought, If it was that close why didn't he just grab the poor thing? He kept on saying the bird was right on top of him and that he was lucky he was wearing tree bark and some moss from an oak. That threw me for a loop and then he said the bird putted and it was all over with. I thought I must have missed the part where he went from turkey hunting to golf but I kept listening. He said the turkey putted and ran away. This wasn't making any sense to me. Although they seemed to be excited about it now, they must not have been too proud of what they were doing because they had said they were wearing masks over their faces.

Although the one bird had escaped, the horror wasn't over. He said after the first bird putted, he quickly ran to another bird that I think he said he located by satellite. I didn't know that was even possible. Finally, I surmised maybe he was hunting near a dwelling and the bird was by a satellite. I also heard him say he thought he saw another full fan. Just when I thought I had heard it all, the guy totally blew my mind. He said he cut at the bird and the turkey blew up right in front of him! I was flabbergasted. First, I couldn't believe the turkey would blow up and, worse yet, it seemed to thrill the guy! After all he had put these poor birds through, and now he had caused it to explode!

I couldn't hold my tongue any longer. I looked the fellow right in the eye and told him I'd heard some tall tales before but his took the cake. He looked at me in amazement. I asked if he thought that anyone would believe that a turkey would explode or that people really shaved beards off of turkeys or hunted them with a gun no longer than your index finger! He just stared at me with his mouth hanging open. I proceed to tell him it was bad enough that he pursued an animal so aggressively just because it had been hammering. And I didn't think that he ought to collect everything the bird had. Not only had he sat on and even crawled up on the turkey, worst of all was when, with one bird whining, he had tried to stab the other with a piece of glass! I said I certainly understood why he wore a mask over his face and that if I had done half of what he had, I wouldn't even show my face in public! The fellow was looking at me like *I* was speaking a different language. I concluded by saying that what probably bothered me the most was how excited he got when he said the bird blew up right in front of him.

By this time, I was raising my voice and had drawn the attention of most of the restaurant patrons when I disgustedly asked, "Who would want to see a turkey blow up right in front of them?" This is when things really got crazy because almost everyone in the restaurant replied in unison, "I would! I would!" In the back of my mind, I could hear music. It sounded like a mix between the theme from *The Twilight Zone* and "Dueling Banjos" from the movie *Deliverance*! As I tried to leave, several people asked where I had seen the blown-up turkeys and if they could hunt them. This was even crazier than before. Who would want to hunt a turkey after it had blown up?

I was headed for the door in a fast walk when a game warden walked in. In all my years of hunting, I never remember being so happy to see the game warden. But that was before I had listened to these rednecks detail their dogged pursuit of a poor bird. I rushed over to the officer and quickly told him, "The three guys in the corner booth chased a turkey this morning and took its hooks and beard and also made it blow up." My heart sank when he looked at them and said, "Congratulations!" and asked if he could weigh it and maybe get a picture.

This time I was running for the door. I stopped long enough to pay my bill and warn the waitress that those guys in the corner were crazy. She replied, "Well they're crazy about turkey hunting, but I hear they are good doctors." I was so totally confused by this that all I could hear was that *Twilight Zone* music.

The music kept playing until it became an irritating buzz. As I tried to sort things out in my mind, I realized the buzzing was coming from my alarm clock. I turned it off and sat up on the edge of my bed. I started putting on my camo and thinking back on my dream. I wondered how many times people had overheard me relaying a turkey tale and what they had thought. As I headed out the door, I decided I didn't have time to ponder it right now. I knew where a gobbler had been hammering it yesterday and I needed to get to that ridge and hoot and with a little luck, I might be able to add his beard to my collection! You might want to try it sometime!

Turkey Hunting Veterans

EXPERIENCE IS THE BEST TEACHER. I don't know who originally penned that adage but I would say they knew what they were talking about. This adage holds true in turkey hunting as well. We in Alabama often take for granted the amount of experience we can gain in a single season. Our long season and liberal limit afford the ardent turkey chaser the opportunity to gain three to four times more experience than most hunters across the country. This being the case, Alabama has more than its share of turkey hunters with a wealth of experience. It has been my good fortune to know a couple of veteran turkey hunters who between them are approaching ninety years of gobbler chasing know-how. If you add in the time amassed by their sons the total begins to approach two hundred years. Now with all that hunting under their belts, when these guys speak you had better listen.

During World War II, two young men from east-central Alabama were serving their country in the Pacific Ocean. Ralph Kelley served in the navy on a destroyer escort, while T. J. Brown was serving as a marine in the same area. While happy to serve their country, both young men looked forward to returning to their native Alabama to once again roam the hills and hollows. Although each man witnessed the horrors of war and survived some close calls, by the grace of God both safely returned home to their families and eventually took up the pursuit of the monarch of the woods, the wild turkey.

Each man loved the challenge of turkey hunting and shared the love of the outdoors with their sons. My favorite story revealed how that Ralph Kelley began taking his son Blake hunting when he was five years old. At the age of nine, Blake began carrying a .410 shotgun. The two would sit side by side and would shoot simultaneously when the gobbler came within range. With Blake shooting a .410 shotgun, his shot may not have even reached the turkey; however, he thought he was killing the birds just like Dad. And within three or four years he was! I remember one year when Blake had taken more turkeys than his dad. Mr. Kelley was asked about this fact and I loved his reply. He stated that Blake should kill more than him because he had taught him all he knew and surely the boy had picked up something on his own!

Examining the hunting careers of these two veterans reveals some truths that both experienced and novice turkey hunters should heed. Calling turkeys is the subject of much attention these days. Calling competitions are only outnumbered by the vast array of calls that are available today. However, the number of calls available is basically irrelevant to these veterans. Although each year there are numerous new innovations in calls, the call these guys use hasn't changed in decades. Their lure of choice is, of course, the box call. Having taken hundreds of turkeys yelping on a box call, they have seen little need for anything else. I've often thought about this as I carry my turkey vest, something else they have little use for, with my two box calls, a push button box, a slate, and numerous mouth calls! Calls should be kept simple.

Having grown up in a time when one was fortunate to have *a* gun that was used to pursue all game, it is easy to see why these guys haven't gotten caught up in the turkey gun craze. Don't come around these pros and expect to find something laminated or synthetic, a ported or even screw-in choke, a shortened barrel or a pistol grip stock. Both hunters shoot an "off the rack" Browning 12-gauge with a full choke. No sling and no special sights, just a front bead. Guns should be kept simple.

During the many years these veterans have been pursuing turkeys, shot shells have come a long way. I dare say that many of the folks chasing turkeys today don't even remember when shot shells were made of paper. These guys remember it well. Of course, the conversion to plastic is sort of overshadowed by the numerous improvements that have come down the pike in the past few years. The best shell to shoot is a topic of much debate among many turkey hunters. The possibilities are almost endless. Copper plated, steel, bismuth, lead, Hevi-Shot, Hevi-13, extended range, Nitro, TSS, and on and on and on. With the nearly endless number of choices available, it is interesting that when you ask these guys what you should use to consistently take tough toms they answer with "#4s." What kind of #4s? "The kind that will shoot well in your gun." It really is that simple. Now both men realize that some shells pattern better than others. However, each one has found that a #4 has been more than sufficient for the job. A few years ago, Mr. Brown had run low of shells and decided to use a gift certificate he had received to purchase some of the new-fangled super shells and see how they would do. Mr. Brown was somewhat taken aback when he placed the two boxes of shells and the fifty-dollar gift certificate on the counter and then had to find an additional ten dollars to cover the purchase! If you ask him what has really changed in shotgun shells, he'll tell you it's the price! Shot shells should be kept simple.

Every turkey hunter knows that complete camouflage is an important turkey hunting accessory. With the multitude of camouflage patterns available today, many people forget that camouflage is a relatively new innovation. Although his son finally persuaded Mr. Kelley to wear camouflage when hunting, the majority of his turkeys were killed while he wore a pair of blue denim overalls! Mr. Brown, on the other hand, does wear camouflage; however, he now does the majority of his hunting from a ground blind. These hunters know what many hunters have learned the hard way. Having knowledge of the woods and turkeys and the ability to remain still will result in more turkeys than wearing the best camouflage available.

At around eighty years of age these hunters began to realize the hills seemed to be getting steeper and the gobbling wasn't quite as loud as it once was. Standing on a ridge and hearing a distant gobble wasn't nearly as exciting as hearing a close-by gobble. Each hunter realized traversing the hills and hollows had become something of a chore. If there were some way to keep the gobblers in close that would sure help out. With a little help from their sons, the two found what is very near to a magic bean for turkey hunting. That bean is actually a tuber, chufa. Both men learned to appreciate the chufa patches their sons planted. The numerous tubers produced underground lure turkeys in and often hold them close by. The chufa patches give the men a great place to listen for gobblers without having to traverse miles of hilly terrain. Many gobblers have lost their lives near the patches.

So, lets recap what these veteran gobbler getters had to say on the subject. Know the woods, know turkeys (as much as is possible), learn to yelp on a box, sit still, let the turkey get within forty yards, and aim for the neck with a shotgun that shoots a good pattern. Everything else is pretty much fluff. When I interviewed this dynamic duo, they were eighty-five and eighty-seven years of age and were still successfully employing these techniques taking five gobblers between them. Not too bad for some octogenarians who were just sticking to the basics. I found a lot of wisdom in their simple approach.

Both of these turkey hunting veterans have now passed away, like we all will. However, I often think of them and their somewhat simplistic yet successful approach to turkey hunting. Although they considered their turkey hunting know-how as simple, I found it to be much more than that. These men were woodsmen, meaning they knew the woods and how to maneuver and use the woods to their advantage. They were students of nature (especially turkeys) and they were teachers and mentors willing to share their knowledge with others. While they were passionate about chasing turkeys, they did not neglect their roles of husband and father. They did not view hunting turkeys as a numbers game. They were ethical hunters who obeyed the rules and regulations and who relished getting to eat the turkeys they killed. They were good role models. It was my good fortune to know them and their families. Life is full of blessings. We need to realize these blessings, appreciate them, and be thankful for them.

A Turkey Hunt to Remember

IN MID-JULY 2016 my life changed forever in that my wonderful dad went to be with the Lord. It was a difficult time; however, his life had diminished significantly due to Parkinson's and a series of strokes. I held his hand and told him I loved him as he slipped into Jesus's arms.

I'm so thankful for the many wonderful memories I have and wanted to share one with you. It's a fun departure from game and fish work but it is a hunting story. Although dad didn't hunt very much, I was able to convince him to go turkey hunting with me once during the Alabama spring season. I must admit I am addicted to turkey hunting and don't understand folks who aren't. Calling in a drumming gobbler is one of the ultimate thrills in life. How someone couldn't enjoy that, I don't know. I just knew if I could get Dad on a gobbling bird, he too would be hooked.

Mother and Dad made the 212-mile trip to my house in Coosa County. It was in the heart of turkey season and I knew where there was a gobbler that had been gobbling pretty well and I hoped I could get Daddy set up on him. We made plans to go the next morning. As I was getting Daddy decked out in camouflage from head to toe, he advised he didn't not want to shoot a turkey but would just like to watch. I told him that was fine and I would be happy to shoot the turkey if we were fortunate enough to call it in. With all of our clothes laid out we turned in with high hopes for the next morning.

We were hunting on the property of a couple of good friends who had graciously allowed me to hunt and fish their property for several years. The road leading to the property was known throughout the area as the ridge road. The road is probably ten miles long and is normally fairly rough. The properties along the road received a lot of hunting pressure. There were two houses on the south end of the road and no other full-time residences on the road. That meant in my law enforcement capacity we spent a lot of time on the road since outlaws loved to "ride" the ridge road.

We arrived at the property and began our walk in. It was a clear morning and not overly hot, which made for an easy walk. We reached the top of a ridge and I told dad to listen for a gobble following my owl hoot. I hooted and a gobbler split the calm morning with a lusty gobble. I told Dad, "Let's go," and we took off toward the bird. As we closed the distance, the bird gobbled a couple of more times, which allowed me to pinpoint him pretty well.

We finally got in a decent position above the gobbling bird. The only drawback in our set up was the only trees we could set against were about fifteen feet apart. I had hoped we would be right together so I could explain what all was happening, but it just didn't work out that way. This being the case I ended up using hand signals and gestures to communicate.

I began calling to the bird and he aggressively gobbled back. Each time he gobbled, I would look over at dad to be sure he had heard it. He would normally nod his head letting me know he had heard the bird. While the gobbler responded to my calls, unfortunately he was being reluctant to come in. Years of turkey hunting had taught me you have to be patient when hunting the monarch of the woods.

Finally, after a lengthy lull in the action, I began to hear walking in the leaves. I could tell the walking was just under the hill in front of me. As I snuggled into the stock of my shotgun, which was pointed toward the sound, I heard another sound. This was a rhythmic sort of a drone-type sound. I could tell it wasn't coming from in front of me but seemed to be off to my right, toward my dad. I slowly turned my head to the right and then discovered the source of the sound. It was Daddy and he was fast asleep!

As I was looking at Dad, I caught movement out of the corner of my eye in the direction where I had heard the walking. I turned my eyes back to the front just as a wild turkey hen topped the rise followed immediately by a second hen. I held my breath and waited for the gobbler I knew was following them. I couldn't help but think the blast from my 20-gauge shotgun was about to be a rude awakening for my dad.

The hens were moving steadily and were quickly closing the distance between us. As I watched, the two birds were on a direct line to Dad. The gobbler still had yet to top the hill; however, the hens were now about seven or eight steps from my sleeping dad. Just then, Daddy snored and the hens erupted. Both of the birds emitted high pitched alarm calls or "putts" and immediately launched into the air. Obviously, the birds did not know what had startled them as they lit in the trees directly above us. In response to all of the commotion caused by the hens, the gobbler responded with a loud double gobble. This racket was enough to wake my daddy who had no idea the hens were setting in the trees above us. Hearing the gobbler, he looked at me and gave me a thumbs-up, totally oblivious to what had just taken place. All I could do was lean back against my tree and laugh. I had hoped for a memorable hunt with my dad and I sure had gotten my wish!

It didn't take long for the hens to fly out of the trees, which startled Dad, and evidently the gobbler also decided to fly the coup, as we never saw him.

That was the only turkey hunt my dad ever went on and I'm so glad we got to share that. Memories are all I have until I get to meet my dad again in heaven. I encourage you to make some memories today. There's no guarantee about tomorrow.

Today, myself and our county game warden, Drake Hayes, went to the same property that the above hunt took place on. We experienced one of the greatest turkey hunts I've ever had. It's a long story but I can sum it up by saying eight gobblers, 173 gobbles, and Drake toting a twenty-pound turkey with an 11-inch beard and almost 1.5-inch spurs to the truck! It was no doubt another memorable day.

Pete's Turkey

ONE OF THE BRIGHTEST SPOTS in my career was working with the TREASURE Forest Program. TREASURE Forest is a program of the Alabama Natural Resources Council that recognizes landowners who are doing a good job of managing the natural resources on their property. Landowners are required to select their primary and secondary management objectives and make accomplishments toward those goals. Once several accomplishments are in place the property is inspected by a wildlife biologist and a registered forester. The inspection form is completed and sent to the TREASURE Forest Committee. The members of the committee (which I chaired for many years) vote to either certify or deny certification. Certified landowners are publicly recognized and presented a nice sign to display on their property. I was a large supporter of the TREASURE Program and I'm proud to say that my county, Coosa, has more certified TREASURE Forests than any county in the state.

Having worked in the majority of the state, I would be hard pressed to tell you how many TREASURE Forest inspections I have performed. It's several hundred. However, there is one inspection that definitely stands out in my mind.

Coosa County Forester Blake Kelley and I had tried numerous times to line up an inspection on a property in the far northwest corner of the county with no success. It was often difficult to mesh our schedules with that of the landowner, a business owner from Birmingham. We once again contacted the landowner and he suggested we might have to meet with his caretaker and view the property. To our surprise and delight he said if we would like he would send us a permit and we could turkey hunt the property that morning prior to the inspection. Evidently the landowner did not realize both Blake and I were turkey hunting addicts. It was one of those times when you did your best to remain calm but almost screamed "Yes!" into the phone. He said he would mail us the permits and the inspection was set.

Years earlier, hunting out of the state vehicle had been a common and accepted practice; however, that was no longer the case. Blake and I decided the chance to turkey hunt the well-managed nine-hundred-plus acres was well worth taking a few hours of leave. When the hunt/inspection date arrived Blake and I were in my personal pickup headed toward the property. We had set the inspection appointment with the caretaker for 9:00 a.m., which gave us three hours to locate and kill a couple of turkeys.

Dawn found us listening with great anticipation. The large property was dissected by a county road, which offered several good listening spots. We quickly got to know the road very well as we traveled back and forth from one end of the property to the other listening. Finally at 6:30 a.m. we heard a single gobble. The turkey was of course on the highest, steepest ridge on the property. However, since he was the only game in town, we began climbing up the side of the ridge. By the time we reached the top, my socks were totally in the toes of my boots and it took quite a while for me to catch my breath. However, we felt good about our location in relation to the bird that was still gobbling.

We found an old logging road on the top of the ridge and quickly set up alongside it and began calling. My initial calls were answered enthusiastically. The old boy was gobbling hard but appeared to be anchored in place. We tried every call we had and every trick we knew. We called while walking away from the gobbler and then hurried back into position. His next gobble revealed he was still in the same spot. Our box call, slate call, and mouth call all received lusty gobbles but the bird stayed put. Finally, after two hours it was getting close to the time of our appointment. Blake decided he was going to attempt to circle around the turkey and see if he might answer some calling from another location. He had wanted to try this earlier but I had persuaded him we would be able to call the gobbler in. I had now been proven wrong, my hands had gone numb from holding my shotgun, and we were quickly running out of time. I knew Blake had successfully moved on turkeys several times before and hoped he would be able to pull it off again.

I continued calling as Blake slipped off the side of the hill. The bird continued to gobble and I knew that would help Blake keep track of where the bird was. A few minutes later I heard a low putt from the direction of the gobbler and figured the bird had seen or heard something he didn't like. I immediately gave a yelp on my mouth call and readied my gun. Seconds later I saw the gobbler's white head coming along the logging road. A few seconds later he was flopping in front of me. I ran to the turkey and was soon joined by Blake. The gobbler was a nice one with an eleven-inch beard and one-inch spurs and tipped the scales at twenty pounds. I offered a prayer of thanksgiving over the bird and we loaded him in my vest and headed off the mountain.

As we approached the truck we saw the caretaker was there waiting on us. We walked up and received a notably cool reception. I was very excited and didn't really understand why the man was looking like he had just eaten a dirty sock. I knew this guy didn't hunt but now I was wondering if he might be against hunting. After I loaded the turkey in my truck, and still seeing the dour expression on his face, I asked him if there was a problem. He responded, "You killed Pete's turkey." I wasn't sure what that meant. I knew this wasn't a domestic turkey so I really didn't understand his meaning. The fellow explained his father-in-law, Pete, had been trying to kill that turkey for five years. Not knowing exactly how to respond and still being pumped with adrenaline I responded, "Well he won't have to worry about it anymore." The man looked as if he had lost his last friend. I asked if he was going to be okay and he replied he would but he didn't know about Pete!

As an avid turkey hunter for thirty-six years I can tell you I have known several turkeys that I spent way too much time on. Many of those have ended up being taken by someone else. While that can be aggravating, I've learned not to lose sleep over it. At the time this occurred this was the most interesting turkey hunt I had had. That combined with the reaction of the caretaker and the fact it was my best turkey to date, I decided to have the bird mounted. Pete's turkey still stands in my den. As a matter of fact, as I write this, I'm looking at the bird right now—and enjoying it all over again!

After the Putt

I DON'T KNOW OF ANYONE who would tell you their favorite call that a gobbler makes is the putt. I've heard a few do it and it normally doesn't work out to well! However, that isn't always the case.

I was hunting on some property just south of Rockford one morning which turned out to be memorable in more ways than one. It was a hunt where I experienced a few "firsts" in my turkey hunting career and those days are often ones you will remember.

After listening on another property and not hearing anything, I decided I would stop by this place and give it a listen. I pulled my truck in the woods road and got out without a lot of confidence. My owl hoot went unanswered and I started to get back in the truck and move on. However, I decided I would try a crow caw before leaving. Lo and behold I heard a gobble and the ole boy wasn't that far down the road. I pulled on my vest and quickly made my way toward the gobbler. Although the road seemed to lead straight to the bird, I knew I would be seen if I tried to take that route. Therefore, I flared off to the west and made a wide arc and then started back toward the road when I thought I was somewhat in line with the gobbler. The way the property lay, I thought I could get back to the road and set up, which would give me a good vantage point. As I neared the road, I heard the now close-by gobbler and realized he was in the bottom straight in front of me.

As I hurried into place just across the logging road, I was thinking I was in a really good position being above the bird. The only drawback was that there was some thick underbrush between me and the bird. I made it across the road and found a good tree to set up against. It allowed me a good shot in the logging road and down the side of the road. I hoped the bird would avoid the brushy area due east of me and come around to the road, which would not go well for him.

I got settled in against the tree and gave a really low yelp, which was immediately answered by a gobble. Luckily, the bird was a little below me and if he would come to the road it would likely be a pretty easy shot. I guesstimated the bird was about eighty yards away and knew by the way he answered he didn't to hear a lot of other calling. My scratching in the leaves was immediately answered by a lusty gobble. I could tell the bird had already closed the gap somewhat and unfortunately he appeared to be moving due north, which would quickly have the thick brush between us. I looked to my left and realized there was about twenty yards of open ground between me and a large, downed log and not far on the other side of the log was the thicket. I didn't know how things were going to turn out but I was looking forward to finding out.

One of my turkey hunting mentors was fellow game warden Earl Brown. Earl was a really good turkey hunter. The thing that I remember that he emphasized the most was that once a turkey knows where you are, you need to play shut up. I have found it to be good advice, although it often isn't easy to adhere to. However, in this case I was doing my best to keep quiet.

Turkeys have a knack for walking wherever gives them the advantage. I guess this could be due to the fact that something tries to eat them every day of their life beginning when they are still in the egg. They are no doubt good at surviving.

The next time I heard this bird he sounded like he was under the hill on the other side of the brushy area, which was straight to my left. And maybe forty yards. That was pretty good except for the fact that I couldn't see him and had no idea where he would pop out. I decided my best bet was to shut up and wait it out.

The bird gobbled again and I could tell he was even closer yet I couldn't see anything. I sat tight and just kept scanning back and forth with my eyes. I could hear the bird walking in the leaves. I reached down beside my leg and lightly scratched in the leaves and the bird gobbled. I could tell he was about as upset at not being able to see me as I was at not being able to see him. I knew he was really close but I still couldn't see anything. I was holding my gun tight to my shoulder and was looking down the barrel that was pointed toward where I thought the bird was. I did not know I was about to experience a couple of firsts in my turkey hunting career.

As I held my breath and watched for the bird, I was somewhat startled by an extremely loud putt. Now in my turkey hunting experience a putt is not something I want to hear since it is usually followed by the sound of a turkey running or flying away. This putt was followed by another just as loud putt. And then yet another. It seemed obvious this bird wasn't running away.

Just as I was thinking I had never heard such a loud and close putt before, the gobbler suddenly flew up and lit on a downed log about eighteen steps in front of me. That was also something I had never had happen before. As I was slowly lining up my front bead on the bird's neck, he again putted and then bobbed his head up and down, obviously looking for the hen that had annoyed him to no end. Although I was pretty surprised, I leveled my bead on his neck and eased his mind by blowing him off the log!

I ran to the bird and placed my foot on his neck. I thanked the Lord for the one-of-a-kind show he had provided. Obviously, his putt wasn't an "I'm leaving" putt, which unfortunately I had heard before. I believe it was a frustrated and extremely loud "where are you" putt. Either way it made for a memorable hunt with firsts of a where-are-you putt and of shooting a gobbler off of a log.

I carried the bird home and started the chore of cleaning him. It wasn't long until I experienced another turkey hunting first when corn began falling out of the bird. Let me pause this story here and make a statement. How anyone who has ever called up a wild turkey can stoop so low as to shoot one over a bait pile is difficult for me to comprehend. I cannot understand what they feel is being accomplished. The best I can figure out is it's an ego-driven thing. I know several folks who are held up as sure enough good turkey hunters who are in fact just outlaw thugs! I have met several of them in an official capacity. We have caught folks in Coosa County hunting in early February when the season began on March 15 and in early June when it had ended on April 25. Not only were they out of season but they were also hunting over bait. It makes me sick. There is no way I would trade the experience of calling in a gobbler for ambushing one over a pile of corn and I have no use for anyone who would. Finding the corn in the gobbler I had killed, I immediately had a plan for that afternoon. It included a lot of walking.

I felt certain there wasn't any bait on the property I had been hunting on; however, you can never be 100 percent sure. However, I had a sneaking suspicion the corn had come from across the county road and that was where I began my search. The property contained a lot of acreage but fortunately it seemed the baiting had been limited to the roads on the property. When I finished looking at the tract, I had samples from nine bait piles! I knew that I rarely saw anyone on the property through the week and surmised that the weekend would be the time to be there.

The more I thought about it the madder I got. Early Saturday morning I hid my truck and eased onto the property just after daylight. I listened for a telltale owl hoot or turkey calling but heard none. The camp house on the property was off the road to the point that I could not see whether or not there was a vehicle there. I had decided I would ease in and see if I heard any owl hooting or calling. Not hearing anything I decided to slowly walk through the property and check some of the baited areas.

Working turkey hunting is difficult in that those you are after are normally totally camouflaged. On several occasions I have walked right past a motionless hunter, which is a little nerve-wracking. Fortunately, on this day the violator made it pretty easy. As I was easing along a woods road, I spotted the camouflaged hunter as he sat in the road looking away from me and toward a pile of corn. What happened next was something I've had happen many times. I walked to within about thirty yards of the young man without him ever looking in my direction. I learned a long time ago not to startle someone holding a loaded gun so I whistled at the man. No response. About thirty seconds later I again whistled a little louder. I had no way of knowing how many hunters might be on the property and I didn't want everyone to hear me. However, it was obvious this guy wasn't hearing me. I whistled a third time and I noticed a slight movement by the hunter. He slowly turned his head and I waved at him and told him to place his gun on the ground. It always amazed me that hunters could not hear my approach and then once they heard me whistling they would slowly turn as if it might be a deer or turkey whistling at them.

I approached the young man and asked to see his hunting license and learned he did not have one. I asked who he was hunting with and he gave me the name of the people who owned the property. I asked where they were and he advised they were still in the bed at the cabin. While I did not necessarily believe him, I had not heard anything that made me think differently and he seemed to be pretty truthful. I was about to see how truthful.

I asked if he had had any luck and he said he had not seen or heard anything. I asked when he had put the corn out and without missing a beat he responded he had put it out last week. I asked if the pile we were looking at was the only one he had put out and he replied, "No, there are several piles." I then explained it was illegal to hunt by the aid of bait and issued him citations for the bait and the lack of a license. I followed by explaining this area would be considered baited for ten days after all the bait had been removed. I clarified that if he removed all the corn today, neither he nor anyone else could hunt until ten days had passed. He stated he understood. I explained his bonds and advised him of his court date and that I would see him there. He pled guilty to both charges.

The Osmose Field

IN THIRTY-SIX YEARS OF WORKING with hunting clubs and landowners I have witnessed many interesting names of stands and fields. Some of the locales are marked with signs while others are listed on maps of the property. Some of the names are easy enough to figure out, such as "the elm tree stand" or "Joe's field," while others, such as "the gypsy wagon" stand, likely have a good story associated with them. I'm sure the circumstances resulting in the names of these places would make for an interesting book. As a matter of fact, I have firsthand knowledge of how one field got its name.

I am certain at this point that you have learned I am passionate about turkey hunting. I do my best to be in the woods every morning of the season. I know several others who also share this passion—or affliction. Although we keep track of how well one another's season is progressing, we really aren't in competition. As a matter of fact, we often share info on gobbling birds to assist one another. Such was the case several years ago. I had been talking with a friend, Brian Walker, a certified wildlife biologist and avid turkey hunter, who was having trouble even hearing a bird. I knew where a bird was gobbling and invited Brian to accompany me the next morning.

As Brian and I stood waiting on daylight, a vehicle approached our location. I was somewhat surprised when I realized the vehicle belonged to our friend and hunting companion, Blake

Kelley. Blake and I both hunted the property; however, I knew Blake had already killed his limit. He exited his truck and told us he was out just listening for gobblers. Did I mention this was addictive? I told him I had been hearing a bird and had asked Brian to go with me. Although he tried to leave, I persuaded him to accompany and assist us. Blake killed the limit of turkeys every year and I knew his fifty years of experience would be invaluable.

I asked Blake if he would do the honors and he let loose with a raucous owl hoot that received an immediate gobble. We hurried up a logging road that led toward the bird and were soon standing in a food plot. We hooted again and pinpointed the bird at about one hundred yards down the logging road. Turkeys routinely walk logging roads in our area so we felt we were in a good position. We closed the distance another twenty or thirty yards and made our setup with Brian looking down the road.

With everyone settled in, I gave a few soft tree yelps that resulted in a booming gobble. Within a couple of minutes, the bird hit the ground. I yelped at the bird and his resounding gobble told us the bird was closing the distance between us. As I listened intently to hear the gobbler drumming or walking in the leaves, I began to hear another sound. Something was moving in the leaves all right but it was directly behind us. I could tell it was closing the gap quicker than the gobbler in front of us, but I wasn't necessarily sure just what it was. Although it didn't really sound like a turkey, I had been fooled before.

I needed to know if we had a bird coming from each direction, so I slowly turned my head as it got louder. Suddenly, I saw it. At first I didn't want to believe my eyes but I was certain I was seeing a flashing yellow strobe light. I then saw the light was attached to a white pickup. I know my jaw was sagging as the truck continued up the road and into the food plot just off to our right. On the door of the truck was a large oval decal that read

Osmose. These were the guys who travel around the area checking the condition of wooden power poles. Many thoughts were running through my mind. Where did these guys come from and why were they here in the middle of our food plot, a half mile from the nearest power pole at six o'clock in the morning? The other more disturbing thought was that they were going to ruin our turkey hunt. I hoped that the driver would realize there were not any poles on this road and would turn around and leave. As I watched the truck stopped. The driver placed the truck in reverse and the backup alarm began beeping and the gobbler began putting! That was the last straw; I jumped from my hiding spot and headed toward the truck, shotgun in hand.

Although I don't think the driver ever saw me, he did hurry out of the area before I had the opportunity to "talk" to him and that was probably for the best! Obviously, our hunt was ruined. Although we laugh about it today, I still recall that morning every time I hunt the area that will forever be known as "the Osmose field."

The Pleasure Was Mine

"I SEE IT!" the fourteen-year-old half whispered and half screamed. The gobbler was coming to my call just as I had hoped. All we had to do was be still and quiet and let him come in. Sometimes that's easier said than done.

While viewing an online turkey forum I was disappointed to learn how many of the participants were bad-mouthing the efforts of state wildlife agencies and the National Wild Turkey Federation to introduce new hunters to the sport. One of the first things that came to my mind was how they got started turkey hunting. While turkey hunting can be a phenomenal personal experience, I have learned to embrace the opportunity to take someone else turkey hunting. I have reached the point where it's about the hunt and definitely not about the kill. That was confirmed again this season when I passed on a gobbler at twenty-three steps in hopes I could call him in the next day for the fourteen-year-old who would be with me. Incidentally, I finished the season without pulling the trigger, although I could have taken four gobblers.

I remember many years ago when I asked an old game warden if he turkey hunted. He responded he used to but he didn't anymore. He told me he had taken forty-seven gobblers when he decided he had taken enough. I did not understand that then, but now with more gobblers than that under my belt, I'm understanding it a lot better.

Prior to the turkey season a dear friend reached out to me and asked if I would take his grandson, Hogan, turkey hunting. I jumped at the chance. Let me tell you taking a kid turkey hunting can be interesting. In Alabama we are blessed with both a long season and a liberal limit, which allows avid hunters to gain a lot of experience in a relatively short amount of time. While some aspects are relatively easy to comprehend, others are hard to understand and even harder to explain. It can be challenging in many ways. Many new hunters do not give enough credence to the turkey's senses of sight and hearing. They often don't understand there likely will not be an opportunity to raise their gun once the turkey is within range. Nor do they realize a turkey can pinpoint their location from hundreds of yards away.

As Hogan and I were waiting on the gobbler to appear, I heard the bird drumming. I whispered that I could hear the turkey. I did not say I could hear it drumming. I knew that was something I couldn't explain, especially with the bird closing in on us.

Turkey drumming can be a hard thing to explain. When you think about it, if you are one of the lucky people who can hear drumming, it doesn't really sound like a drum at all. I have learned many people can't hear drumming, while others can hear it a remarkably long way. I have heard turkey hunters make the statement if you can hear a turkey drumming, he is close enough to shoot. I can tell you that isn't necessarily true. While walking along a logging road with my avid turkey hunter friend, Blake Kelley, he abruptly stopped and whispered to me he heard a turkey drumming. Listening intently, I didn't hear a thing. We eased a little farther down the road and spotted a strutting turkey that was at least one hundred yards from us. We quickly set up and called to the bird. As he got closer, I began to hear him drumming. I will agree that for most folks drumming is an up-close event.

So how do you explain drumming and what is it anyway? I tell new hunters that drumming is a noise a gobbler makes normally when with hens or when what he thinks a hen is near. I consider it sort of a love language that's more subtle than a gobble. When asked what it sounds like, my best answer is to mimic the sound. However, one drumming description always comes to mind. Heads up: The upcoming story may sound familiar!

While working as the area wildlife biologist on the Coosa Wildlife Management Area one of the many duties I performed was the enforcement of laws and regulations. During turkey season this normally consisted of checking hunters as they entered or exited the area. We tried to avoid disturbing hunters in the woods unless there were extenuating circumstances, such as if they were sitting over a pile of corn!

I would often set up and check licenses and permits and firearms to be sure they were unloaded. Upon being stopped, hunters' responses ranged from being genuinely happy to see someone out there working to being highly annoyed at the inconvenience. The vast majority of stops were no problem, including those that resulted in citations being issued.

One spring morning I was checking vehicles at a major intersection when I heard a vehicle approaching. I motioned for the driver to stop. As I stepped to the window I noted the driver was shaking his head and was obviously upset. Reading someone's demeanor was a very necessary skill in my line of work. I quickly realized his anger was not directed at me and I went about checking his firearm, licenses, and permit. Finding everything in order I asked the loaded question, "What's the problem?"

"I've never been so frustrated," was the quick reply. The distraught hunter began to describe the morning's hunt, stating he had heard a gobbler on the roost at first light and had set up near him. The bird aggressively answered his calling and flew down. He said he could tell it was getting closer until "it" happened. Having encountered a lot of hunters, I had heard my share of horror stories concerning hunting on public land. I knew it was not uncommon for an unethical hunter to attempt to crawl between a hunter and the turkey he was calling. I hoped that wasn't where we were headed. The hunter said the turkey was closing the distance and he was readying himself for a shot when he heard it. He again became disgusted when he said evidently someone got stuck down in the hollow below him. I'm sure my face revealed I didn't fully understand what he was saying. He said all of a sudden all he could hear was someone revving up their truck engine off in the distance. He said the turkey quit gobbling, or at least he couldn't hear it over the *vroom, vroom* of the truck engine. He said every time he made a sound all he could hear was *vroom, vroom*. He said he couldn't believe someone revving their engine had ruined his hunt. Finally, totally frustrated, he stood up and a gobbler flushed from less than twenty yards and flew away. He said he was so frustrated and startled he had to sit down and calm his nerves before walking out.

Those experienced turkey hunters reading this have already figured out what was happening. There was no truck down in the hollow; the revving engine was actually the drumming of the strutting gobbler coming to what he thought was a turkey hen! It was all I could do to maintain a straight face. I told the fellow I hated that had happened to him and maybe he'd have better luck next time. As he prepared to leave, he suggested I go to the area he had described since there was probably somebody stuck down there that needed assistance. I told him I would check it out. With that he revved up his engine and drove away. Therefore, when a new hunter asks what drumming sounds like, I just rev the engine and say, "It sort of sounds like that!"

As I said earlier, I knew I didn't have time to explain drumming to Hogan seeing how I had now spotted the gobbler closing in on us. I whispered to Hogan to watch for what looked like a baseball moving through the woods. Hearing his exclamation of "I see it!" excited me almost as much as the bird excited him. As the bird closed the distance I told him to get the bead on the bird's neck as we had previously discussed. I asked if he had it on him and he said he did. I scratched in the leaves behind my back and the bird extended his neck. I said, "Shoot him," and a young man's love affair with the monarch of the woods began. It was a fine gobbler with a ten- inch beard and one-inch spurs. We knelt over the bird and thanked God for his creation and for what we had just experienced. Hogan thanked me over and over.

New hunters can be a lot of fun. I know I have been abundantly blessed having hunted and taken many gobblers through the years. I am thankful for the folks who were willing to take me to the turkey woods and teach me. I am again blessed to be able to pass on the passion. Congratulations, Hogan, and thank you.

Generating Gobbles

ONE OF THE MANY REASONS I love turkey season in Alabama is that, for the most part, the weather is very favorable. It isn't very consistent, but it is usually pretty nice. On many occasions I have hunted when it was cold enough to see my breath (which has cost me more than one gobbler), and I've hunted when the sweat was in my eyes. While even those days aren't terrible, normally the weather is good. However, there is one major exception. They don't call this area Tornado Alley for no reason.

No matter where you live, I assume you understand the utter destruction caused by tornadoes. Interestingly of late, we have experienced several wintertime tornadoes. However, March and April are pretty tough months for the twisters.

A few years ago, we experienced what was by far the worst non-tornado windstorm I have ever been a part of. The weather service said we had ninety-mile-per-hour straight-line wind. When you add hail into that mix, you experience some tremendous destruction. Not only were there thousands of trees blown down and homes severely damaged, thousands of trees were killed by the wind-blown hail. I have never seen anything like it and would rather not ever see it again.

As it turned out, I was having a tremendous turkey season. As you have already read, I surely don't have to kill a turkey to have a great hunt. I don't hunt for the limit; I hunt to enjoy the hunt.

I know several good turkey hunters who love to hunt like I do but do not understand how I can pass on a gobbler from time to time. This had been a tremendous season and I could have already taken the limit.

Even though things were in a mess, you still have to turkey hunt if the season is open. The windstorm had added another obstacle that I normally don't have to contend with. Due to the storm knocking down the powerlines, where I was hunting I could hear two generators running. Or I probably should say I could barely hear because of two generators running. Once again when you enjoy turkey hunting like I do, you put up with whatever comes along. Two days earlier I had enjoyed a tremendous hunt on the property. I had two big gobblers and two hens at a distance of twenty-five yards. I could not get a clear shot at either gobbler. Those who haven't hunted turkeys a lot might not understand not being able to get off a shot at such a close distance. However, I will not attempt what I consider an iffy shot, and turkeys have an uncanny ability to survive close encounters.

The gobblers were fired up. The pair had gobbled ninety-two times by six o'clock. By 7:00 a.m. I had counted 102 gobbles. When our encounter ended, my gobbler clicker read 110 gobbles.

Although it was difficult to hear, knowing the birds were there, I set up in the same area. The humming of the generators in the distance definitely took away from the experience. As I sat there calling every once in a while, I was writing this article in my mind. I remembered once telling a friend of mine that I often write articles in my head and he responded that it looked like I had done a lot of erasing! Just because I am hair challenged, there was no call for such a remark!

I was working on the conclusion when movement caught my eye. Looking up I spotted a gobbler as it was flying across the field straight at me. A jake with a three-inch beard landed about fifteen yards in front of me! The young bird was definitely looking hard for the hen he knew was somewhere right there! He stayed within gun range for thirty minutes. I have never shot a jake and don't ever plan to. A light yelp on my mouth call brought the bird even closer. I was a little surprised when at ten yards the bird offered a light yelp of his own. He followed that with a nervous cluck and then walked away. Did I ever see the big gobblers? No. Did I have a tremendous hunt? You better believe it!

The Difference Between Thinking and Knowing

I THINK HE'S BEHIND US.

I think he's going to come down that road.

I think I should call—shut up.

I think I should gobble.

What is the allure of turkey hunting? I think it may be the difference between thinking and knowing. I know of nothing in hunting that can humble you like a turkey gobbler.

When I hear someone who says they always know what a turkey is going to do, I know they either don't know what they are talking about, have trouble telling the truth, or haven't known the turkeys I've encountered.

I have witnessed some weird turkey behavior in my thirty-five-plus years of turkey hunting. Recently a close friend asked if I would take his grandson turkey hunting. While I very well know the many challenges of taking a new turkey hunter into the woods, I was glad to take the young man hunting. On one of our hunts he commented about how smart turkeys were. I took that opportunity to try and explain that turkeys were not "smart" per se. However, turkeys were survival experts. Literally from the time they are in the egg, turkeys are widely sought after by a multitude of predators.

If I had a dollar for every time I thought I have wrongly predicted what a gobbler would do, I would have a lot of dollars!

Ohio Monster Turkey

"**YOU EVER THOUGHT ABOUT** hunting in Ohio?" That was the question my friend Blake Kelley posed to me. I told him I hadn't really thought about it. He explained his hunting partner could not make the trip and he would enjoy some company on the twelve-hour ride. I told him it sounded good to me.

Blake was one of my turkey hunting mentors. Having started hunting with his dad at the age of five, Blake has logged over sixty years in the turkey woods. His dad, Ralph, was a dedicated turkey hunter who began hunting the birds as soon as the season was opened back in the 1950s. Coosa County was one of only a few counties in Alabama that held a remnant population of wild turkeys and never had turkeys restocked.

Plans were made and we readied for a long road trip. Weather is always a gamble and this trip was no different. Our first morning was one of those mornings when you question why you ever left your home state. The wind was blowing and the rain, while not pouring, was pretty steady. We failed to hear anything that even sounded like a turkey. Furthermore, the tract of land was little more than a razorback ridge next to a paved county road that had a fair amount of traffic. To say we were disappointed was an understatement.

We returned to our hotel and found our outfitter and inquired about other tracts of property. He assured us there were several turkeys on the tract we had been on; however, we were ready to try somewhere else. He gave us directions to another tract and we decided to try it the next morning. The property was again a small tract. So small in fact that we decided one of us would hunt it and the other would go back to the first tract. It was decided I would hunt the "new" tract. This meant Blake would drop me off and then drive the twenty or so miles back to the first tract. This required he would be dropping me off pretty early.

The next morning found me standing in the dark waiting on it to get light enough for me to ease into the woods. Unfortunately, it was once again a windy morning but it least it wasn't raining. The cloudy conditions took away the sunrise I had hoped for. My first owl hoot received no response. I eased down a little further and gave it another try. While the howling wind made it hard to hear, I felt certain I heard a gobble below. I quickly picked a path I felt would let me close the distance between myself and the bird. I moved approximately one hundred yards toward the bird and slid in beside a large oak tree. I pulled my old beat-up Aluminator from my pocket and laid it in my lap. I then gave a light yelp on my mouth call. After getting no response, I yelped a little louder but all I heard was the blowing wind. I found my striker and tried the Aluminator. When it did not receive a response, I decided to try to get a little closer.

One of the things about hunting somewhere you've never been is you have no idea about the lay of the land or how birds will respond, how much they've been hunted, and so on. While I have been fortunate to take a lot of turkeys I am far from an expert turkey hunter. However, there is something I believe to be true: If you can consistently kill turkeys in Alabama, you can kill a turkey anywhere!

As I got up and started moving down a small hill, it once again began to rain. GREAT! I had passed a pop-up blind that the outfitter had told us was there for deer hunters. As the rain got harder, I decided to go back and get in the blind and hope the rain would let up.

I unzipped the back of the blind and tried to climb in. I quickly realized my large frame coupled with my vest on my back was not going to be easy to get through the small opening. I removed my vest and pushed it in in front of me and slid inside. Fortunately, there was a small seat inside. I unzipped the front and side window and laid my shotgun on my vest, which was on the ground. I had arrived just in the nick of time as the bottom fell out. With the rain pouring, I was thankful to have the blind but aggravated that the weather was definitely messing up the hunt. Thankfully the heavy rain did not last long. When it subsided, I leaned over to the opening and cut on my mouth call. Although the rain had stopped, the wind was still blowing and I didn't hear anything. I continued to call when the wind would give me the chance.

As I sat and lamented about my bad luck, I heard the unmistakable sound of a twig breaking just outside my blind. I instinctively pulled my facemask up over my face. As I eased my hand, down a gobbler's white head appeared at what seemed to be about six feet from mine!

One of the main reasons I hunt turkeys is for moments like this. The up-close, intense situation is one of the most exhilarating things one can experience in the woods. If you have never had a gobbler drum so close that you actually felt it, you may not understand what I'm talking about. If you've never had an unsolicited gobble almost blow your hat off, you may not be very excited right now. If you've never felt your heartbeat so loud in your head that you were sure the bird was going to hear it then you have missed out! However, if you've had one or all of those things happen you know how I felt as the bird strutted past me with my gun on the ground in front of me. As I began to hear my heartbeat in my head, I realized I was holding my breath. I was frozen as the bird slowly strutted by. His full fan told me he was an adult, although I never saw his beard. Thankfully he was moving from right to left; however, there was nothing between us but air.

I knew any movement on my part might send the bird into the next county. However, I also knew I would not kill the bird with my gun on the ground in front of me. As I tried to calm my breathing in an effort to avoid hyperventilating, I was thinking if he would just turn slightly to his right, his fan would block me from his view. As if on cue, he slowly turned to the right. I immediately, in one fluid motion, retrieved my gun and brought it to my shoulder. I knew that with a bird that close the load of heavy shot from my trusted 20-gauge would be like shooting a slug. As the gobbler turned back slightly to his left, I placed the bead on the back of his head and pulled the trigger. Fortunately, he dropped straight to the ground and did not flinch.

I climbed out of the blind and walked the twelve steps to the gobbler. It was a beautiful bird. As is my custom, I removed my hat and knelt over the bird and thanked the Lord above for his creation and for letting me be part of it. He is an awesome God and I had once again been overly blessed.

As I had done many times before, I rolled the bird over to check his beard. It was a nice one. I estimated it to be twelve inches, which would equal the longest beard I had ever found on a bird I had killed. I then looked at his legs and my mouth fell open.

I need to pause here and tell you that I have this thing about killing turkeys with only one spur. As a matter of fact, the first turkey I ever killed did not have a spur on either leg. It weighed eighteen pounds and had a nine-and-a-half-inch beard and was spurless! The Osceola I killed in Florida had one spur. It was a good spur but was missing its counterpart. An eastern I killed in Louisiana, one spur. You get the picture. So, as I looked at this bird's legs, I would not have been surprised if he only had one spur. However, I was definitely surprised at what I saw. It was easily the longest pair of spurs I had ever seen. I felt certain they were two inches long.

I texted Blake and told him I had killed a turkey and it had two-inch spurs. There was some hesitation before he replied with "I'm on my way." I carried the bird out close to the road and hung him in a tree by his spurs. They were extremely impressive and easily the largest I had ever taken.

Blake soon arrived and couldn't believe his eyes. We took several pictures and discussed the hunt in detail. We dressed the bird and went to look at another small tract the guide had told us about.

When we finally found the tract, the entrance was right on the edge of a fellow's yard and he was out mowing his grass. He stopped his mower and we stepped out and encountered him. We introduced ourselves and told him we were from Alabama and had come to Ohio to try to kill a turkey. The man's reply was one neither of us has ever forgot. He replied, "If you can't kill a turkey here, you suck at turkey hunting!" We walked into the woods and struck up a gobbler. Unfortunately, he had a bunch of hens with him and we soon learned that, evidently, "we suck at turkey hunting!"

We ended up leaving with only the one bird but Blake returned a couple of weeks later and checked Ohio off of his national list!

Games Turkeys Play

As I sat in the humid woods listening to a distant gobbler, I could not help but think about the games turkeys play. Oh sure, turkeys are wary and often extremely hard to kill. However, they also possess an aggravating sense of humor and I believe they really enjoy messing with us!

To start with, calling a turkey's departure from a roost tree a "fly down" is often somewhat of a misnomer. Sure, some turkeys fly down like they are supposed to, others not so much! One thing I always find a little funny and a lot sad is the number of people who I hear say, "Can a turkey fly?" Among the general public, evidently a fairly high percentage do not think turkeys can fly. It seems to blow their mind when you tell them a turkey can fly at fifty-five miles per hour. I digress.

Supposedly, the "norm" for a turkey is to pitch off of a limb and soar to the ground. I have learned that many gobblers will simply step off of the limb and hit the ground. Often without making a sound! Others will launch from their perch and glide for a couple of hundred yards!

You cannot trust a turkey to do what it is supposed to!

Gobblers have a whole bag of tricks and believe me when I tell you they will stoop pretty low!

One of the most aggravating games is obviously one of their favorites and that's ping-pong. Getting ping-ponged is when a turkey gobbles a quarter mile to the south and you head toward him. He continues to gobble until you get within about two hundred yards and he shuts up. Then his brother or cousin takes up the mantle and gobbles within fifty yards of where you started. He continues to gobble until you turn around and head back toward him. You slide in beside a good tree and offer a yelp and the first gobbler gobbles from where you just left from. They continue this until they have worn you down to the point you can't chase them anymore. If you have never experienced that you haven't hunted enough!

Another game that resembles ping-pong is the yo-yo. The yo-yo is where you hear a gobbler. You call to him. He closes the distance between you. You think he is getting pretty close and then he gobbles back where he started. He will do that a couple of times until he gets tired of you.

Can a turkey do that? Will they?

A turkey will stoop pretty low. They may turn their head away when gobbling to make you think they are much farther away than they are. That way you will walk right up on them and they will fly out so close that it makes you pee your pants a little bit. I'm telling you sometimes they act like they don't even want to get shot! They will stoop low enough to send out a jake to test the water. They know all of their heads look alike! I've had them intentionally break a stick just to get me to move so they can see my surprised expression as they run off!

On many occasions I've had gobblers yelp like a hen just to try and fool me.

You may not know it but turkeys possess incredible measurement skills. Not only do they understand the distance from one stop to another, they also know how long your stride is. By knowing both of these, turkeys are able to gobble just before you reach your vehicle to leave!

I call this their "You aren't leaving are you?" gobble! They often wait until you are reaching for the door handle and they then gobble again to see if they can lure you back.

I am reminded of hunting squirrels as a youngster. We did not have any wild turkeys or deer at that time in northwest Alabama. Therefore, my uncle Reed was an avid squirrel hunter and introduced me to the activity. Since I was not old enough to drive, my mother would sometimes take me to the woods and come back and get me a couple of hours later. One day while I was hunting, a bird flew over and pooped on my arm. I actually found it pretty amusing and once I got home I called Uncle Reed to tell him about it. I have never forgotten his response. I finished telling him the story and he asked if I had got any squirrels. I told him no. He then said that when the bird went home and they asked it if it had got any, it could say, "Yes, I got one!"

I can't help but think a lot of turkeys do the same thing. After they have pranked me to no end, they return to the others and say, "I got one!"

Drumming Gobblers

AFTER AN HOUR OF GOOD GOBBLING, the woods had gone silent. Old Superglue had stuck to his guns once again. I had named the turkey during the previous season due to his aggravating habit of staying in the tree until he saw a hen. I had crawled up under the bird on one occasion and watched him gobble over one hundred times. He stayed in the tree until after 7:00 a.m. Only when a hen came walking in did he fly down.

This morning was no exception. The turkey had gobbled over one hundred times before a hen finally walked up and the ole boy flew down. Once he hit the ground, I started pouring on the calling. As I had hoped, the hen didn't appreciate my offering and we aggressively exchanged words with the gobbler chiming in regularly. A second gobbler also responded; however, Superglue appeared to be closing the distance between us.

My then nine-year-old, Caleb, was sitting on my left side facing the gobbling bird. When the bird gobbled at about eighty yards, I had Caleb get his gun up and pointed in the direction of the bird. Unfortunately, the next gobble revealed the hen had gained the upper hand and the gobbler was now about 125 yards away. Soon thereafter the woods went silent. I knew it would be tough to wrestle the gobbler away from the hen. However, I had hope that with Superglue preoccupied, the other gobbler might slip in.

As we sat silently, I heard that sound that says, "OK, I'm here. Where are you? I heard a drum."

Drumming is that mysterious sound that makes the hair on the back of your neck stand up and tells you that the gobbler is pretty close. I've heard many turkey hunters state that if you can hear drumming, the turkey is close enough to kill. Of course, that depends on how well you can hear drumming (some people can't) and how well your gun patterns. I recall a hunt when my hunting partner, Blake Kelley, and I were slowly walking down a woods road when he stopped and whispered, "I hear drumming." Listening as intently as possible, I couldn't hear anything. We eased to the side of the road and there, one hundred yards away, stood a gobbler in full strut. We crawled to the nearest cover and hurriedly set up. After a few soft yelps, the gobbler closed the distance to about sixty yards. At that distance I could also hear the drumming. Unfortunately, a hen was with the ole boy and was doing her best to lure him away. The ole girl decided she needed to run me off and began walking straight to me. While that didn't help me much, she did pull the gobbler to where Blake could put the ole boy's drumming to an end.

Many times, the drum is the only thing to let you know a gobbler is anywhere around. That was the case this year when Caleb and I locked horns with Superglue. The woods had been silent when I whispered to Caleb that I heard a turkey drumming and to get ready. The second gobbler that I had heard earlier had evidently decided to check things out. I spotted the gobbler's head as it popped over a ridge about thirty yards from our setup. I whispered to Caleb that the turkey was coming from the right. The turkey was steadily closing the distance. I again told Caleb the turkey was coming from the right side and asked if he could see it. With the big gobbler at fifteen yards, Caleb turned his head and exclaimed, "I see it!" and the gobbler exclaimed, "Putt, putt, putt!"

As I leaned back against the tree, I recalled a morning a few years ago when I sat at the exact same tree and turned my head only to hear the resulting "putt." Like father, like son. While some might think that wasn't a good day, I beg to differ. Cherish the times spent with loved ones. They are way too few.

It's the Hunt

DURING A PAST SEASON I had the opportunity to have my youngest son accompany me on a couple of hunts. We are so richly blessed to have a friend who owns a great deer and turkey property. I had already had a great season in that I took a fourteen-year-old on his first ever turkey hunt and he killed a fine gobbler. That bird was one of three that had come in to the call and I hoped we would be able to possibly get on those birds again.

I went to the property and immediately heard a gobbler sounding off. I quickly made my way toward the bird. I soon realized there were at least two birds gobbling. Having hunted the property for thirty years, I think I know every nook and cranny or trail that one can take. I quickly crossed a hayfield and was now in the woods adjacent to where the birds were gobbling. I quickly picked out a tree to set up at while the birds gobbled like crazy.

As I stepped to the tree, I spotted a gobbler standing in the field about fifty yards from me. Of course, in this type of situation the question is always whether or not the gobbler saw me. The next gobbles told me the bird I had seen was not one of the pair that were supplying the almost nonstop gobbling. I slid down beside the tree and hoped for the best. As I prepared to call to the hard-gobbling birds, I could not help but wish I had my son with me.

Let me take you on a little aside for a minute. As I mentioned, I love turkey hunting. I've been pursuing the monarch of the woods for around thirty-five years. Just as I was developing my passion for the activity, I asked an old game warden if he turkey hunted. He told me he used to. That got my attention. He went on to say he had killed forty-seven gobblers but no longer had the desire to kill one. I remember wondering how someone loses the desire to take part in one of the most exhilarating activities one could ever experience. It was somewhat baffling. Later, I spoke with another old game warden. He told me that he used to hunt turkeys but he didn't shoot them anymore. He went on to tell me that well known call maker, Mr. M. L. Lynch, used to come and hunt with him and his wife on a regular basis. He said Mr. Lynch would normally always give them a box call when he came. I was shocked when he told me he had sixty-two of the now famous boxes! Once again, I was baffled that someone would just quit hunting turkeys.

As I sat listening to three gobblers tearing it up, I could not help but wish I had my son or my fourteen-year-old friend with me to take one of these birds. Several years ago, I began to feel some remorse after taking a turkey. I knew that bird would never be able to put on the show again. I realized it's about the show. It's the hunt not the kill. I think it has something to do with proving that you can take the bird. Now that I've done that nearly a hundred times, I am quickly getting to the point where taking a bird is not the goal. I still love the hunt. I have no problem with someone killing turkeys but I am content to work the bird. Pulling the trigger isn't necessary.

Back to the story. I gave some soft yelps that were immediately and enthusiastically answered by all three gobblers. It wasn't long until I could tell the gobbler I had seen earlier was coming in. I knew in order to take the bird I needed to turn to my right. As I contemplated the move, I had to address the question of whether or not I wanted to kill the bird. I did not move. The bird walked by off to my right at twenty-three steps. The birds gobbled a total of 121 times. Yes, I count them. That afternoon, I told my son I had been on some hard-gobbling birds and we needed to go there in the morning.

As soon as we got out of the truck, we could hear the three birds tearing it up. We quickly made our way toward the birds. Due to where the birds were, we could not get into a really good position; however, you never knew what might happen.

The birds were aggressively gobbling at everything I offered; however, they were reluctant to move close enough to the woods for a shot. After 171 gobbles, they finally exited the field walking right past a couple of trees I had set up at many times in the past. I told my son we needed to be set up at those trees in the morning.

The next morning the conditions were great. It was about fifty degrees, clear and with no wind. We were standing at the end of the field waiting on the gobbling to ensue. And we waited and waited. Finally, we heard a bird way off in the distance. We made it to our setup site and I tried everything I knew. Nothing. We finally gathered up and started back to the truck. We had walked about 250 yards when we stopped and my son burped loudly. Two turkeys gobbled back toward where we had been. Of course, we turned around and went back toward the gobbles. My calls once again went unanswered. I told Caleb to burp and they didn't answer that either. You just can't trust a turkey!

Third Pass Is the Charm

I COULD WRITE A BOOK about the boom and bust of turkey hunting. Although I have been richly blessed with a tremendous property to turkey hunt on, that definitely doesn't mean they gobble every day! This occurrence was no exception. The landowner called me to give me a turkey report and said there were two gobbling their heads off behind his house. I told him I would check on them the next morning. I did and they didn't. I did not hear a peep on the whole place. Same weather conditions as the previous day. Not a peep!

I went back the next morning and decided to try the other side of the property. I got out of the truck and heard a gobble that was off the property. I then heard one behind the house where he had said they were two days ago. I got in the truck and drove around to the house.

As soon as I got out the turkey sounded off. I gathered my gear including my camera and camo net that I set up when I take pictures. I walked up a field road with the turkey gobbling about 125 yards to my north.

I decided to set up on the side of a small opening between the gobbling bird and a large hayfield with hopes of calling the bird in, but if not, hopefully one would come in the hayfield and afford me the opportunity to get some pictures.

The bird was gobbling good while I got net set up and my calls out. I was a little surprised that I did not hear any other gobblers but was happy I was in a good position on this one.

I gave a low yelp on my Thunderdome friction call, which was immediately answered. I laid the call to the side and just listened. The gobbler continued sounding off. Eventually, I heard another gobbler probably two hundred yards behind me. It wasn't long until I heard the first bird fly down. I gave a light yelp, which was immediately answered. I adjusted my position.

I was fortunate in the fact this bird had not been roosted on the hill directly in front of me, an area I had not so affectionately named "No Kill Ridge." Birds roosted on that ridge had won almost every battle we had engaged in. It was perfectly designed for turkeys in that it was shaped so you could not get on the ridge with the birds without them spotting you, even in the dark! I've tried! Interestingly, the only gobbler I've killed with a twelve-inch beard was killed on that ridge. As memory serves, I've killed two on the ridge!

This bird was luckily roosted just across a drain from no kill on a smaller hill. My hope was he would drop off in the drain and walk down it as I had had birds do before.

In just a couple of minutes after the fly down, I saw the gobbler's head appear just above the grass at about forty-five yards. I tightened my grip on my gun and snuggled my cheek against the stock of my 20-gauge. I don't know how many turkeys I've killed with this gun, but it's the majority of them. It didn't take long to understand I didn't enjoy getting the snot knocked out of me every time I shot a bird. I found the National Wild Turkey Federation Jakes Remington 20-gauge at a local gun shop and scooped it up. This was way before Tungsten Super Shot was the rage. This gun has always shot Hevi-Shot #5 great. Although I killed a bird at maybe fifty yards from where I was currently sitting, I always tried to limit my shots to a maximum of forty yards.

The gobbler had been moving west, which was going to bring him straight in front of me. I followed the bird with my bead on his neck as he was searching for me. Unfortunately, instead of coming on into the field, he seemed to be veering up toward No Kill Ridge. This was not good.

I was constantly judging the distance and kept saying to myself he was at forty-five yards. When he broke into the open, I was having a battle in my mind whether or not to shoot him. It wasn't much of a battle in that I have never taken what I thought was anything but a shot that would surely take the bird cleanly. The excitement of taking a turkey is not at all worth the risk of wounding and losing a bird. I assume every turkey hunter has misjudged a bird as I have, hence the one killed at forty-six steps, but if it's risky, I'm not taking the shot. If the bird walks away, it gives me a chance to hunt him again!

I have hunted this property for a long time and I was beginning to believe I might have dealt with this bird before seeing how stayed at least forty-five yards out as he walked a semicircle around me. I guess since I had quit calling he was a little suspicious when he didn't see the hen on the edge of the opening where he knew she was. I followed him with the bead as he walked to my right. As he neared the wood line, he stopped and ran his head up looking hard. I once again judged the distance at forty-five yards. I strongly considered taking the shot but hesitated.

I watched as he walked into the woods. Another turkey gobbled maybe two hundred yards below us at the end of the hayfield and he responded. I figured this hunt might be finished but I definitely wasn't ready to throw in the towel. I yelped and both birds gobbled. I could still see the gobble until he got out to about seventy-five yards. He went on to the field and he and his buddy gobbled at each other.

I decided to check my yardage judging and removed my range finder from the vest and checked some ranges. I checked the area where I first saw the bird and it showed it was forty-five yards. When he moved toward No Kill Ridge and was straight in front of me, he was at forty-seven yards. When he stood at the wood line and looked at me, he was forty-three yards. I found a little solace in having judged the distance correctly; however, I knew I would feel better if I could call him back.

As I contemplated my next move, I remembered I had lugged my camera with me and I might could slip around and get some shots of the birds in the hayfield. However, I also knew trying to move on multiple turkeys that close often didn't turn out well. As I was trying to decide, the two birds gobbled and I could tell they were in the woods to my left. This helped me decide not to try a move.

Within a minute I spotted a gobbler that appeared to be walking the same path as the early gobbler had walked. Exactly the same path. I sat with my mouth hanging open as the single gobbler came out of the woods at forty-three yards. It was as if the bird was walking in his own tracks as he walked the same semicircle around me. When he was about forty-seven yards, he turned around and walked back the same path back into the woods again. I watched until I lost sight of him. I leaned back against the tree and contemplated the chances of something like that happening.

I offered another call and quickly received a couple of gobbles. The birds were toward the hayfield but not all the way down in it. Once again I debated whether or not to give up the hunt and try to capture the birds on camera. Once again I knew it would be difficult to get in position without being spotted. As I considered my options, I spotted movement to my left.

At about seventy-five yards I could see a turkey moving but could not identify it. That is until it went into a strut. As I watched, a second gobbler came into view and then a third!

A very light yelp got the attention of the strutting bird who gobbled in conjunction with at least one of his friends. If they would come straight at me, which might happen since they were in a woods road, they would walk right across where the first bird had stood at forty-three yards. I hoped the bird would not again take the same path that kept it just out of range.

Seeing how the birds were moving my way, I felt it best to play shut up. When I say *birds*, there were now three longbeards coming my way. I tightened the grip on my gun and held my breath.

As the lead bird got closer, I spotted a fourth gobbler in the line. Luckily it was a fairly warm morning so I wasn't worried about my breath creating steam. I don't want to talk about how many times I have had that happen! However, when you have four sets of eyes moving in on you, with one set that had already walked this path multiple times, you can't be too careful!

The lead bird was approaching the forty-three-yard spot and I was wondering if there was something the first bird had spotted from there and if that was about to happen again. When the bird reached the spot he came out of his strut and my heart began to sink. However, when he and bird two kept walking, I started concentrating on making the shot. They took a few more steps and I knew he was within range. Although I did not think the beard on this bird was as thick as the first one, it was still plenty long enough. I put the bead on the ole boy's neck and dropped him at thirty-four steps. The bird hit the ground and did not flop.

While I kept watching the downed bird, I was also noticing that bird two and three had both run about ten steps. Bird four had not gotten within fifty yards of me.

Instead of jumping up and running to the downed bird as usual, I kept the bird covered and watched the other two. I first thought the birds were going to jump on the dead bird as I have had happen only once in the past. When I was convinced the bird was down for the count. I laid my gun to the side and grabbed my camera and started taking the photos of the two remaining birds. Although they were spooked, they did not act as if they were in any hurry to leave. I yelped with my mouth call and both birds gobbled.

At this point, seeing how these birds were hesitant to leave, I felt certain the fourth bird in this setup was the first bird who had walked past me basically three times and he had decided to lead these less savvy longbeards to the slaughter.

When I got to the bird, as is my custom, I knelt over the bird and thanked the Lord for allowing to experience this tremendous part of His creation. I looked at the bird's beard and found it was not like any other I had ever taken. The beard was 9.5 inches long and thin. However, it wasn't thin because it wasn't a full beard but because it was stuck together. It was as if it had been greased and stuck together.

Talking Vendor

ONE OF MY STRONGEST PASSIONS is turkey hunting. For many years I did my best to hunt every morning of the forty-five-day spring wild turkey season. Although work and bad weather would sometimes get in the way, I usually averaged hunting about forty mornings each spring.

After rising early every morning for a few weeks, I would begin to feel the drain; however, not going didn't cross my mind. I recall one morning late in the season when it was particularly difficult to get out of bed. However, you never knew which day would be the day a gobbler decided to gobble his head off. I was soon up, dressed, and in the truck. As I approached the four-way stop in the middle of Rockford, I noticed the Coke machine at the gas station. I decided I could put some caffeine to good use.

For anyone not from the South, it is a Coke machine. It is not a soda or a pop machine. Once while at graduate school at Mississippi State, I had to explain to several foreign students (Wisconsin, Michigan, etc.) the proper beverage nomenclature. I tried to explain to them how asking someone in the South if they wanted a pop could very well result in them getting popped—upside the head! I told them the proper sequence was to ask, "Do you want a Coke?" Of course, they protested, "What if you want some brand other than Coke?" Bless their heart. I explained it is a two-part question. You ask, "Do you want a Coke?" If they say yes, then you ask what kind of Coke they want. I digress.

During this time, there were two gas stations in Rockford, the county seat of Coosa County. They were located directly across the street from each other. The Majik Mart was a convenience store/gas station and the other was a Texaco gas station. The Texaco closed at 5:00 p.m. and the Majik Mart at 10:00 p.m. Therefore at 4:30 a.m. both places were snoozing like the rest of the town. I pulled up in front of the Texaco, dug around in the truck for some change and approached the only outside Coke machine in town.

I put in the required change and suddenly somebody says, "Hello." At that time and still today, I carry a pistol at all times, including en route to the turkey woods. And now I found the gun in my hand and pointed at a Coke machine that was now saying, "I'm a talking vendor. Please make your selection." Thank goodness this was before every corner had a surveillance camera or I'm certain the tape would have gone viral! At first, I was shaking like a leaf and about to hyperventilate. Then I began to laugh hysterically. Of course, I looked around to make sure no one had witnessed my armed encounter with the voice in the Coke machine. I can't recall how the hunt went that morning but I can report I was wide awake and I never stopped and visited the talking vendor again!

You can't make this stuff up!

Turkey Thugs

"PHILLIP'S ALREADY GOT THE LIMIT," my friend told me. We were only two weeks into the season.

Knowing Phillip to be an ethical turkey hunter, I knew that was quite an accomplishment. Taking the limit in my home state of Alabama normally means spending a lot of time pursuing the monarch of the woods. Statistics show that only 4 percent of turkey hunters in the state harvest the limit of five gobblers. Unfortunately, those stats are gathered from those hunters who provide the legally required harvest information. The percentage on that is difficult to attain; however, I venture it isn't close to the number of those hunting in the state. Furthermore, our stats fail to capture those who do not stop after taking the limit. Yes, they are out there. Several of them.

Any time a reduction in the limit is mentioned, it is met with outrage from the hunting public. The truth is, we don't necessarily need a reduction in the limit as much as we need an adherence to the limit!

Harvest records in Alabama reflect that only 3–4 percent take the limit. Unfortunately, this does not capture those who routinely exceed the bag limit on both a daily and seasonal basis. Contrary to popular belief this does happen on a regular basis.

Before you get the idea that every turkey hunter is some type of outlaw, that definitely isn't the case. I once had an old crusty game warden give me his take on hunters. He had worked for many years and had encountered thousands of hunters. He said 10 percent of hunters leave home looking to break any game law they can. Ten percent will not break the law under any circumstance. The other 80 percent will only break the law if given the opportunity! While I think that percentage may be high, understand what he is talking about. I have caught many violators who have told me they didn't know why they did what they did. Several were very embarrassed by their own behavior. Many of these folks would not fit in the thug category.

It may be the person who got one had a second gobbler that hung around after his brother had been shot. In a past season, I killed one of three gobblers and the other two continued to strut and gobble. I could have easily killed another one and probably all three of them. Many people who heard that story commented most people would have killed the others as well. Comments such as those really bother me. I have spoken to many hunters who did not know I was a conservation enforcement officer who opening admitted taking multiple turkeys in one day. Some seemed dismayed when I commented I would pass up shooting a gobbler if there was a likelihood of killing more than one turkey. One told me there was no way he would ever pass on a "natural double."

Why do folks feel compelled to exceed the limit or take turkeys in other illegal ways?

Where I live good turkey hunters are held in high esteem. I have often said if you can consistently kill mature gobblers in Alabama you can kill one anywhere. There is no doubt in my mind that we match wits with some of the meanest turkeys anywhere. They are often really tough. I have spent the whole season on one turkey and did not take him. Yet, for me it's about the hunt. When I do take a gobbler, it is quite a sense of accomplishment. I feel I've beaten him at his game. I respect turkeys.

Many years ago while I was in college I was a certified bowhunting instructor. One of the key points we taught was that you owe it to a deer to be able to make a quick killing shot. I once made that statement to an old bowhunter who immediately took exception to it and said he did not see how you were respecting an animal if you were trying to kill it. I did my best to explain that I felt it was unethical to take an iffy shot that might result in a wounded and long-suffering animal. He still didn't agree, which was his prerogative.

I have reverence for turkeys. They are the ultimate woodland survivors. I find them a formidable adversary. Even after taking many of them, it is still a thrill to call one in. When it quits being a thrill, I will quit doing it! I respect them enough that I will not take a risky shot.

Does that mean I have never wounded a turkey? Well, actually, to the best of my knowledge I have not. Have I ever missed one? Oh yeah!

I have a problem with today's guns and shells that claim you can kill a turkey at seventy to eighty yards. To me, the challenge and accomplishment of turkey hunting is getting the bird within forty yards. Can I kill one farther out than that? Yes. But I'm in it for the challenge. Many times, I have passed on a turkey that was well within range but was covered by brush or was in a position where I didn't think I could make a clean kill on them. I've had hunters tell me you can't kill them if you don't shoot. I respond that it's not all about the kill for me. It's the hunt.

Many who make themselves out as great hunters are in fact successful outlaws. Several come to mind. The renowned turkey hunter I apprehended killing a gobbler and a hen by the aid of bait six weeks before the season opened comes to mind. The man was widely known as a turkey hunter. I know how he kills them.

He's been caught again since then. As has his son. Unfortunately, the apple doesn't fall far from the tree.

The fellow who killed sixteen gobblers in one season in an effort to win a biggest turkey contest. He didn't win and the turkeys and legitimate sportsmen definitely lost. The fellow who I was told had killed eighteen gobblers. I checked him the next morning and found he had killed another bird. This was prior to mandatory reporting. When I asked how many he had killed he quickly replied that was his fourth, which was one below the limit. I've checked many hunters who had their fourth bird.

I have found many "hunters" whose best call appeared to be cracked corn, wheat, or scratch feed. I have often made the comment that I don't see how anyone who has ever called in a gobbler could get any satisfaction out of sitting and watching a pile of corn and shooting a gobbler that comes to it. Why not just shoot a chicken?

I have met many quality people who are turkey hunters. This has been especially true with my association with the National Wild Turkey Federation (NWTF). However, there are always bad apples.

How do you eliminate bad apples? Don't honor them. Condemn what they do. Report them.

I love to turkey hunt. I'm proud to admit it. I admit it's addictive and I've been hooked for a long time. I lack the words to explain just what it's like to hear the morning come to life. Standing on a ridge with anticipation high is a certain kind of exhilaration. And then, when a resounding gobble splits the morning calm, it gets me going just thinking about it.

It was my privilege to serve as the Assistant Turkey Project Leader for Alabama for five years. That carried with it the opportunity to serve on the NWTF Technical Committee. I met many fine folks through that association. Again, I admit I'm all about turkeys.

I love turkey hunting because I can hunt them how I prefer as long as it's legal. Personally, I hunt the morning and I want to call in a gobbling turkey. I have many friends who are excellent turkey hunters and who employ many different methods. I have no problem when Blake puts the sneak on a turkey or when Phillip ambushes one on a trail.

When your state possesses a good turkey population, a long season, and a generous limit you end up with a lot of good turkey hunters. That is definitely true in Alabama.

Stereo Gobbler

SEVERAL YEARS AGO, I spotted a gobbler on the gas pipeline right-of-way that traverses my property. Although he was a few hundred yards off of my property, past experience told me that he could possibly be called in. My then fourteen-year-old son, Justin, and I donned our camo and headed for the back of the property to give it a try. I must admit I was a little surprised when my first loud yelps were answered by a distant gobble. I'd learned that this long-distance calling could often be a waiting game, so I settled in and called sparingly.

As we sat motionless waiting on the gobbler, I heard a drum. It was faint at first, then louder. I told Justin to get ready. *Vroom!* I heard it again louder, then again and again. I desperately scanned the woods but could not spot the drumming bird. Then I heard it again this time; however, it sounded different, rhythmic even. My excitement quickly turned to embarrassment as I realized the drumming was actually the bass beat from a car stereo traveling down the state highway half a mile from my home! I fell back against the tree and laughed as Justin also realized I'd been fooled by the "drumming."

As I sat contemplating that there should be a law against stereos that will sterilize a rat at fifty yards, I again heard a *vroom*. Although I'd just been fooled, my turkey hunting instincts dictated that I immediately scan the woods. There, thirty-five yards in front of me, stood the adult gobbler in full strut. I whispered to Justin. Unfortunately, his gun was pointing to the left of the bird and I knew it would be difficult for him to get a shot. As I debated what to do, the bird came out of his strut and began that "something's not right here" shuffle. I'd seen that look before and I took the gobbler. I told Justin that I was sorry he didn't get to take the bird, but he did come away with a pretty good story!

You Suck at Turkey Hunting

I HAVE BEEN FORTUNATE that I have had the opportunity to chase turkeys in several states. Based on my limited experience and the vast experience of some hunting friends I will say that it seems to us that if you can consistently kill turkeys in Alabama, you can kill one anywhere. That is not being boastful. As I mentioned in other stories, we have a long season and a ton of turkey hunters. Our turkeys are hunted hard and have been exposed to everything in the book. I feel this is often not the case in many other states.

Years ago, Blake Kelley, his dad Ralph, and our friend Alan Williams traveled to Texas to hunt turkeys. I had never hunted with a guide service before. I found it interesting when we met with our guide on the evening before our hunt and he asked if we had killed any turkeys thus far in the season. We looked at each other and quickly came up with a total of fifteen gobblers between us. He replied that it sounded like we knew what we were doing. Within a couple of days, we had proven to him that we did. That is everyone except me had proven that to him. I returned to Alabama empty handed. Hey, I didn't say we always killed a bird. If I had a dollar for every hunt that I didn't kill a turkey on I would have a lot of dollars!

My friends Blake Kelley and Phillip Neighbors are on the quest to kill a turkey in every state where they exist. I've not set that goal but do enjoy going to other states when I can. Many years ago, Phillip was one of my 4-H kids in that he took part in the 4-H wildlife and forestry programs. I served as an assistant coach for the wildlife team and Blake served as an assistant coach for the forestry team. I was nominated for and won a national 4-H instructor award, which came with a trip to Washington, D.C., for my wife and myself. I must admit I was pleasantly surprised. Having lived in a rural area all of my life, I wasn't sure I would enjoy a trip to the big city. Seeing how Coosa County has ten thousand residents and one traffic light in the entire county, I wasn't used to the hustle and bustle. At the awards banquet we had a reception where the heads of many organizations came by.

One of the folks present was Rob Keck, who at the time headed up the National Wild Turkey Federation. He came over and introduced himself and asked where I was from. When I told him I was from Alabama he told me that when he was in college, during his spring break he went to the Coosa Wildlife Management Area (WMA) in Alabama to hunt turkeys. He said he had camped in the Horse Stomp campground and had walked from the campground and killed a gobbler. He said that was the first gobbler he had taken outside of his home state of Virginia but since that time he had killed a turkey in every state that had them. I told him that was impressive and that it was a small world. His look told me he didn't understand what I meant. I told him I was currently the wildlife biologist on the Coosa WMA and I was in Horse Stomp campground on a regular basis! Mr. Keck was the first person I ever knew to have completed the national slam; however, Phillip and Blake are well on their way.

A few years ago, Blake invited me to go with him to Ohio in search of a gobbler. We made the twelve-hour drive, located our hotel, and met our "guide." The fellow was actually a deer guide who allowed out-of-state hunters to turkey hunt on their own on his deer leases. If possible, Blake and I would rather pay what some would call a trespass fee which allows us access to the land and lets us do our own calling. The Ohio hunt was somewhat odd in that the tracts we had to hunt were very small and in close proximity to houses. We went and looked at a couple of spots and decided we would definitely need to split up. Blake took me and dropped me off on a small track and he then headed to another. The weather was definitely not the best. It was windy with a light rain. At daylight I offered an owl hoot; however, all I could hear was the howling wind. I eased down an old logging road and during a lull in the wind I hooted and thought I might have heard a gobble. Unfortunately, the wind and the rain both picked up, which didn't allow me to hear anything.

I eventually came upon a ground blind and seeing how it was raining pretty good I decided to duck into the blind and wait on the weather to clear up. Luckily there was a chair in the blind so I sat in the chair and laid my 20-gauge shotgun on the floor. I unzipped the window and whenever there was a lull in the wind I would yelp on my mouth call. Eventually the wind and rain let up and the sun actually came out. I offered a string of yelps and decided I would get out of the blind and see if I could get anything to respond. As I pulled my camo jacket on, I heard a stick break right outside of the blind. As I turned and looked out the window, a gobbler's head appeared at a distance of about fifteen feet! The bird was in a strut and walking from my right to my left. I was shocked. Rarely had I ever had a mature gobbler that close.

I slowly eased my right hand down and gripped my 20-gauge. The bird was still strutting to my left when I raised the shotgun to my shoulder with one hand. (I love the 20-gauge for this reason.) I was able to slowly get my other hand on the forearm. I put the bead on the back of the bird's head, which was about twelve steps from me. I pulled the trigger and the bird crumbled. I got out of the blind and ran to the bird. It was one of the few turkeys I have ever killed that did not flop. Of course, I usually don't let them get to within twelve yards!

I slowly rolled the bird over and checked out the beard and spurs. I immediately knew the spurs were by far the longest I had ever taken. My first thought was they were two inches long. As it turned out they were one and seven-eighths inches and the beard was a thick eleven inches. I got on the phone and called Blake and told him I needed him to come and get me and my gobbler with the two-inch spurs! Blake eventually showed up and the back-slapping and high-fiving ensued.

Blake had not heard anything where he was and was ready to try another tract the guide had told us about. We took care of my bird and met with the guide and got directions to the other tract. We headed to the property. As we neared what we thought was the property line we encountered an old guy on a riding lawn mower. We exited the truck and introduced ourselves to the man and told him we were going to property beyond his house in hopes of killing a turkey. The fellow told us that shouldn't be a problem seeing how he saw turkeys there all the time. Obviously, we were glad to hear that seeing how we had heard a combined total of one gobble all day. The man asked where we were from and was amazed to learn that we had come all the way from Alabama to try and kill a turkey. He left us with a line we have never forgot. He said, "Well if you can't kill a turkey here, you suck at turkey hunting!"

We eventually did hear a bird on the property. We quickly got set up and I began calling to the gobbling bird. Although the bird gobbled several times and we felt certain it was closing the distance between us, we eventually heard some hens and they evidently sounded better than we did. As we dejectedly made our way back to the truck I looked at Blake and said, "Well I guess you know what this means." He gave me a confused look and I said, "You suck at turkey hunting!" He really appreciated that. I didn't bring that up too much on the twelve-hour drive back to Alabama. However, I have used that line from time to time since. Seeing how Blake has forgotten more about turkey hunting than I ever knew, he usually laughs at that. Usually!

A Low Gobble and
a Loud Click

WHEN I WAS LEARNING how to deer hunt, I had a fellow tell me something that I have found to be very true. He said if you spend a lot of time in the woods you are going to see things that people will not believe. He then continued, "And you are usually better off not to try to tell them." Having spent a tremendous amount of time in the woods both for work and pleasure, I have observed a lot of hard-to-believe things.

I learned a long time ago that it is hard to predict what a turkey might do in the woods. Sure, over time you learn to anticipate what a gobbler might do, but you can never be sure. Anyone who tells you they always know what a gobbler will do either hasn't hunted very much or has a problem with telling the truth!

I readily admit I've had many gobblers surprise me. Those surprises run the gamut from the bird that pops up in the direct opposite place than where you thought it would to the gobbler that flew in and lit on a limb right above my head. However, one of the most memorable events I've ever experienced was on a hunt I shared with my hunting partner, Blake Kelley.

Although Blake is only nine years older than me, he was literally turkey hunting before I was born. It's a really sweet story. When he was five years he was accompanying his dad on turkey hunts. Not too long after that he was literally hunting alongside of his dad and shortly after that he was hunting on his own. It was the beginning of a passion that has yet to subside! If you have the opportunity to take a kid hunting, do it. Hunting needs it, turkeys need it, and in all likelihood the kid needs it!

Blake and I hunted together a lot, as they say, "back in the day." He was a turkey hunting mentor and I benefitted greatly from his tutelage. We shared many memorable hunts together and killed a lot of gobblers. Several of those hunts are chronicled in this book. I believe one thing that contributes to Blake's tremendous success at turkey hunting is that he consistently hunts almost every day of the long Alabama season and in several other states as well. We have often discussed how fortunate we have been to live in a state that has a long spring season (normally over forty days) and a liberal limit of five gobblers (now reduced to four). This combination allows us to amass a tremendous amount of turkey hunting experience in a relatively short amount of time compared to those in states with short seasons and low limits. We are richly blessed to be able to spend that much time in areas with lots of gobblers. It's a great classroom.

Several times, Blake and I would be set to hunt in the morning; however, I would wake to rainy or windy conditions, which made hunting difficult to say the least. However, I would soon learn that the weather conditions did not affect Blake's desire to hunt. On several occasions when I would ask if he still planned to hunt despite the weather conditions he would again tell me about the time in '92 when he got his fifth gobbler on the last day of the season in a driving rainstorm! While I know and understand that the turkeys are out there no matter what the weather, I still decline to venture out on some wet and windy days.

I remember well a rainy and windy spring morning when Blake arrived at my house at 5:00 a.m. As we headed to my hunting club property, he again related the story about getting his fifth gobbler on a morning much like this one! We arrived at our listening spot and exited the truck. As the sky was trying to lighten up and during a lull in the wind, Blake hooted. I think we were both a little shocked to hear a distant gobble. We quickly developed a game plan, which included trying to get to a nearby wildlife opening. Anyone who has spent a lot of time in the turkey woods or who has driven through the countryside where turkeys are known to frequent knows that turkeys are often found in open areas on a rainy day. My personal theory is that the rain causes a lot of movement in the woods, which probably wreaks havoc on a turkey's great eyesight. In addition, rain is loud in the woods, which also upsets the turkey's ability to hear. Therefore, turkeys like to get in the open so they can better see what is going on. Hey, it's a theory.

Blake and I headed for the opening in what was a light rain and probably ten- to fifteen-mile-per-hour wind. We arrived at the opening and Blake offered another owl hoot. The responding gobble told us the bird was close and we needed to get set up. Blake looked it over and decided we needed to set up to the left of our current position, which would allow us to shoot across the opening. Unfortunately, there were no large trees around the perimeter of the opening so we slid in against a couple of small trees and got set up.

Blake told me to yelp to the bird. I gave a loud yelp, which was immediately answered. He held up his hand letting me know we didn't need to call anymore. As we sat with bated breath but did not hear another gobble, Blake gave me a head nod and I yelped lightly. It did not get a response. As I was learning, once the bird answered your call, he knew where you were and you probably didn't need to load him up with a lot of calling.

As we sat scanning the edge of the wildlife opening, the gobbler eased into view. Little did I know I was about to experience something that I have only witnessed once in my long turkey hunting career. The gobbler eased out a little farther and lowered his head and gobbled. However, it was the quietest gobble I had ever heard. If the earlier gobble had been a ten, this gobble was maybe a two. We were about fifty yards from the bird. A normal gobble at that range would have blown our hats off. This one was barely audible. After the fact, we coined it a low gobble, something I have never encountered since. As Paul Harvey would say (for those of you old enough to know who that is), the rest of the story is pretty good.

We were set up maybe five yards off the edge of the opening. Unfortunately, I had a small bush in front of me right on the edge of the plot. The turkey slowly began easing down the edge of the field. I had my gun up and on him but he was still just a little out of my preferred range of forty yards. As the bird moved to the left, I had my bead on its neck; however, it was behind the bush between us and I was afraid to take the shot.

Blake whispered, "Shoot." I desperately wanted to shoot but could not get a clear look at the bird. Blake again whispered for me to shoot. I could hear the urgency in his whisper. I whispered back that I couldn't. Blake was sitting to my right and holding his 10-gauge single-shot shotgun, with which he had taken many gobblers. I only needed a step or two for the bird to clear the bush and was praying he wouldn't see anything that might mess things up. However, as is often the case in turkey hunting, there would soon be another factor entered into the situation that would change my way of thinking.

As I kept my bead on the bird, Blake backed the hammer on his shotgun, and the corresponding *click* sounded like a hammer hitting an anvil. At least to me it did! With that inspiration, I did something I had never done before in my short turkey hunting career. I leaned to my right and once my sights cleared the bush, I centered the bead on the gobbler's neck and pulled the trigger. The bird immediately hit the ground and started flopping!

I jumped up and ran to the bird. As was and is my custom, I knelt over the bird and thanked the Lord for the experience. I then looked at Blake and asked, "What was that?" He knew what I was referring to. To the best of our knowledge, in our nearly ninety years of combined turkey hunting experience, this is the only time we have either one experienced this low gobble. Our best guess was the bird did not want to be heard by some rival gobbler. Once again that is only our theory. When you turkey hunt for a long time you come up with a lot of theories! Turkeys just do you that way!

Nothing but a Nub

WORKING ON A WILDLIFE MANAGEMENT AREA (WMA) was interesting. As you might suspect, an area that is open to the public draws all types of folks. This is true for the deer season much more than for the turkey season. However, the Coosa WMA has always been known as a good turkey hunting area. Therefore, it always drew a good crowd. I quickly realized this during my first year of being assigned to the Coosa area. I begin work in January and therefore got to work one gun deer hunt on the area. The gun deer hunts were quite the affair with an average of over a thousand people participating! At times it was more than a little nerve-wracking.

I had been there for two months when the turkey season came around. I quickly learned this was a much different yet just as intense situation. One of the first things I noticed was that by opening day of the turkey season the Horse Stomp campground was full of out-of-state turkey hunters! It was not uncommon to have hunters from ten or twelve states in the campground. Of course, these were on top of the large number of locals that hunted what many of them called "the reservation."

It didn't take long for me to learn that many of the local folks hunted the area regularly during both the deer and turkey seasons. One of those folks was a fellow named Mr. Looney. Mr. Looney had twin sons that he brought with him during the deer season. However, he normally hunted alone during the turkey season. I would often see him on the area during the turkey season and we would discuss how his hunt had gone. I was relatively new to turkey hunting and was always interested in listening to the old-timers in hopes of gleaning some tidbit that might assist me. I didn't know how long Mr. Looney had turkey hunted but I figured it was a long time seeing how he was pretty old. I wasn't sure of his age but he had to be at least in his forties! Yeah, that used to seem old.

My favorite memory of Mr. Looney is of the day I checked him at the end of the Weaver Road. The Weaver Road was on some of the Kaul timberland that was in the WMA. It was primarily made up of old-growth longleaf pine and was good turkey habitat. I knew the area fairly well and knew I had seen Mr. Looney's truck parked in there several times.

I could tell the man was agitated as he rolled up to my roadblock. He quickly exited his Toyota four-wheel-drive pickup truck and came over to me. He exclaimed he had never been so frustrated on a turkey hunt. As I said earlier, I was still fairly new to turkey hunting; however, I had been enough to know that turkeys could definitely frustrate you. However, I would soon learn a turkey wasn't the problem!

He dispensed with any pleasantries and jumped right into his story. He told me the road he had been on and I told him I was familiar with it. He said his truck was parked there at the end of the road where it could be plainly seen. Obviously, this was a sign that someone was hunting in the area and other hunters should move on. However, that had not kept another hunter from parking just down the road and setting up just across the hollow from him. Of course, this was a very regular occurrence when folks were hunting public land. However, I have never forgotten how he described the situation. He said the fellow across the hollow had a slate call. Just in case you have picked up this book up by mistake and do not know what a slate or friction call is I will briefly explain. Although we commonly refer to them as "slate" calls, in reality they can be made of several different types of material. You basically have a flat piece of material that you hold in your hand and you move a striker or peg across the flat piece to make a turkey sound. The strikers are normally about six inches long and can be comprised of several different materials. By pulling the striker across the slate you can produce many sweet turkey sounds. I carry at least two slate calls in my vest every day. My Thunderdome call is my go-to for close-in work! The friction call is great for purring so lightly you can barely hear it to raucous cutting and even putting. I love it. Back to his story.

Mr. Looney told me he had never, in all his years of chasing turkeys, heard anyone call as much as this guy who had come in on top of him! He said there was not a minute that morning that the guy wasn't calling. He again said he had never heard anything like it! He was shaking his head and was really upset. While I knew how upsetting something like that could be, I was finding the way he was describing it more than a little humorous. However, I just thought it had been humorous. Mr. Looney looked at me and said, "When that fellow got there he had a striker that was a foot long and when he left it wasn't nothing but a nub!" I was about to bite a hole in my lip trying to keep from laughing!

I learned that Mr. Looney passed away a few years back. I always enjoyed talking with him and considered him a friend.

Stick to the Plan

TURKEY HUNTING IS VERY OFTEN a reactive situation in that you react to what a gobbler gives you. If he seems to favor a particular call, you keep throwing that one at him. If he responds to silence, you give him silence. If he wants to fight, you give him a gobble, and so forth. However, from time to time, you end up patterning a turkey to the point that you develop a plan for taking the bird. Patterning a turkey takes time and persistence.

I should pause here and warn you that you *can* spend an entire season on a turkey. This is where turkey hunting often changes from a pursuit to an all-out assault on a bird. A bird that you've become obsessed with. A bird with a brain the size of a marble that knows your next move before you do! A bird that you lie awake at night trying to figure out. A bird...but I digress.

Many times, I have come up with a sure-fire strategy to take a difficult gobbler. This type of intense effort is normally reserved for those gobblers that develop the irritating trait of walking (or sometimes running) away from hen calling. Unfortunately, this often can become common near the end of the season and/or in areas of heavy hunting pressure. These gobblers often survive the season by implementing this most aggravating technique. One such gobbler had eluded my hunting partner, Blake Kelley, and me for three consecutive days. Do not misunderstand. I have hunted many turkeys much more than three days without taking them. Much more than three days!

On this bird, each day we had gotten in what we felt was good position on the lone gobbler and each day the ole boy gobbled good on the roost, then flew down and walked directly away from us. Our most earnest pleas went unanswered except for the occasional "I'm walking off now" gobble. After the third morning of throwing everything we had at the bird, we decided it was time for a new strategy. A plan was developed. If the gobbler was in the same general area in the morning, I would set up down the hollow while Blake set up above the bird as we had on the previous days. The plan was for Blake to begin calling and then I would call from where the bird had gone to on the previous days and hopefully the bird would walk right over me.

So the plan was in place and predawn found us once again on the ridge listening to the ole boy bellow out the gobbles. The plan was put into action and I hurried into position as the turkey gobbled on the roost. I hooted to let Blake know I was set up and I heard his first low yelps. I snuggled in against the large oak and judged distances and located possible shooting lanes. The gobbler hit the ground and gobbled. I heard Blake yelping once again and knew it wouldn't be long until the bird would be fleeing his calls and walking into my lap. I gave a light yelp and immediately heard Blake give a loud *cluck* that was followed by the blast of his 10-gauge. I sat in disbelief for a few seconds and then made my way up the hollow to where Blake stood over the fine gobbler. My first comment was, "Well it's evident that you didn't stick to the plan!" He then explained how the bird had pitched off the roost and landed just below him on the ridge and one set of yelps was all it took to bring the bird to thirty steps where a cluck finished the deal. I think there is a saying about best-laid plans.

A highlight of each turkey season is when my good friend and fellow wildlife biologist, Phillip Blake, comes for a visit and hunt. Phil and I attended graduate school together and have kept in contact over the years. Our visit often contains a lot of deep thinking concerning the proper management of different species and discussion of how the more we learn the more we understand that wildlife management really is an art more than a science. Fortunately, we are normally able to work in a couple of hunts as well.

Due to his busy schedule at Portland Landing Hunting Reserve, where he was working at the time, Phil arrived at my house with only two days remaining in the season. Unfortunately, the next morning was not one of the best for turkey hunting. The wind was gusting to twenty-plus miles per hour and it was raining. Add to that the fact that my four-year-old son, Caleb, had awakened with a bad cough and my wife had decided it would be best if he stayed home with me. All things considered, we had a great morning viewing video that Phil had recorded earlier in the season. By noon the sun had come out and Caleb was doing fine. Although there was still a brisk wind, we decided to go and peek into a wildlife opening on the gas pipeline that traverses my property. We eased up and peeked over the hill and spotted a large gobbler scratching in the chufa plot. Although I had watched several gobblers in the field prior to the season, this was the first one that I had seen there during the season. I immediately began formulating a plan to take the gobbler.

We hurried back to the house and donned our camo. I related to Phil that I had tried to call this turkey off of the adjacent property earlier just to have him go the other way. I told him I thought it would be best if I went down the pipeline below the bird and let him go back to where we had seen the bird from and he and Caleb could call to the bird and I would be in place to try and call him in if he decided to come my way. I also mentioned that he might want to video the whole thing as well. Phil gathered his equipment while I got Caleb into his camo. I told Phil I would crow caw when in position and he could respond with a hawk call if the bird was still in the field.

I hurried into position and crow cawed. After receiving no response, I decided to ease down the firebreak and set up and call. I was still easing when I heard the shot, which was quickly followed by a second blast. I hurriedly climbed the hills and made my way to the two camo-clad figures on the edge of the pipeline. The fact that they were both sitting on the ground with no turkey in sight confirmed my fear. Phil explained there had been two gobblers in the field instead of one. He had watched the birds walk toward the side of the pipeline and then lost sight of them. Only a couple of minutes had passed when Phil decided to lean over and look down the edge of the right-of-way. At the same time, a large, bright-red head appeared over the hill only fifteen yards away. The hunter and the bird were each caught off guard but the bird did a better job of gathering his wits than the hunter did. After he finished relating the events, I then jokingly asked him, "What am I going to have to do to get someone to follow the plan?" We then agreed that when you're chasing gobblers, you always have to expect the unexpected.

A famous quote speaks of the best-laid plans of mice and men. I think an appropriate paraphrase would be:

The best-laid plans of a camouflaged man
May work well or may totally fail
Just keep in mind it's the memory that will count
Whether he flies away or you carry him out
Don't give up, give it your best
Just remember you've been blessed
To match wits with the monarch of the wood
And win or lose, it's all good.

Turkey hunting is very much like life in that you really don't know what is coming next. You may think you know, but we are often proven wrong. This was brought home to me recently in a way I could not misunderstand. A normal trip to the dermatologist revealed some spots that turned out to be melanoma. This unfortunately turned into leptomeningeal disease. There is no cure. I've likely enjoyed my last turkey hunt, which really upsets me. However, as I look back, I have been so blessed by God to have been able to hunt the wild turkey for so many years, I can't feel anything but blessed.

Turkey hunting has been a large part of my life. I thank God for allowing that. I'm not sure what things will be like in heaven. It will be paradise. Therefore, turkeys will have to be a part of it! If you want to find out, you need to choose Jesus as your savior so you will get to see. Do it today. I sure didn't see this diagnosis coming. Our days are numbered. I praise the Lord for the many blessings he has bestowed upon me. I bowed over every turkey I killed and thanked the Lord for the experience. Don't forget to do that. God bless.

All Over Again

IT WOULD BE AN ACCURATE STATEMENT to say I am an avid turkey hunter. It's pretty much on the verge of an addiction. I try to go each day of the season if possible. There's not much better than spending the morning in the woods and hearing things come to life. Adding in a gobbling turkey is the icing on the cake. When you can spend this time with a cherished friend or loved one, it's that much better.

During the past season I had the opportunity to have my youngest son accompany me on a couple of hunts. We are so richly blessed to have a friend who owns a great deer and turkey property. My mind goes back to a time over twenty years ago. My friend had built a new shooting house overlooking a wildlife opening on the property and invited me to take my son there to try to shoot a deer. We settled into the shooting house and began waiting on the deer to come out. While we were waiting we discussed where to shoot a deer. Fortunately, a deer finally came in the field. We got the rifle propped in the window and he began trying to get the deer in the scope. With me reminding him about where to place the crosshairs, he eventually told me he had things lined up. I told him to slowly squeeze the trigger. Obviously, my slow and his slow were two very different speeds. The rifle roared and I watched as the deer bounded away with its tail waving, apparently unscathed. Like most young shooters do, he immediately asked me if he got it and while I had my doubts, I told him we would have to go and see.

We made our way out of the shooting house and moved to where the deer was standing. Luckily, there was still a good bit of daylight. We searched the ground thoroughly and did not find any sign of a hit. I hated to have to tell the young boy it looked like it was a clean miss. He did not seem to be too bothered. We went to Mr. Randy's house and having heard the shot he was waiting to hear the story. He asked Caleb, "Where's your deer at?" Caleb did not reply. I told Randy he had shot at a big doe but we could not find any blood in the field. Randy asked him if he missed the deer and the seven-year-old responded with a question of his own. He asked, "Would a deer bleed if you hit it in the foot?" Randy answered that he didn't know and Caleb quickly responded, "Well then that's where I hit it!" I must admit I was surprised and impressed that he came up with that answer. Then he learned about a deer hunting tradition. Mr. Randy explained that when someone missed a deer it was a tradition that they had their shirttail cut off. This was extremely upsetting for a seven-year-old. Mr. Randy removed the shirttail and later put it in a frame and hung it in the shooting house. To the best of my knowledge, it's still in there.

Fast-forward seventeen years. Turkey season finds me and Caleb just below the same food plot, listening for gobblers. Hearing one bird in the distance we decide to set up on the edge of the shirttail food plot. I get set up and Caleb is about ten yards off to my left. Caleb is right-handed but left-eye dominant. Therefore, he shoots left-handed. If you've never turkey hunted with someone who is left-handed I can tell you the way they set up to shoot is totally different.

I had offered several yelps that received no answer. Finally, I cut and a gobbler gobbled not that far away. The response to my next call told me the bird was coming in. Pretty quickly the bird gobbled just on the other side of the wildlife opening. I saw his white head as he peeked up and pulled it back down. The bird came into the field and was on a pretty straight line toward us. I knew if he kept on that path he would afford Caleb a shot. With the bird in view at about fifty yards I did not want to call to him. He kept coming and I could see Caleb adjusting his gun. I scratched in the leaves and the bird looked my way but did not stop walking as I had hoped. *Boom!* I watched the bird as it ran out of the field, apparently unscathed.

Caleb said the bird ducked his head just as he shot. I told him they often did that.

I saw Randy a few days later and he asked if we had had any luck. I told him the story and he told me to tell Caleb that his knife was sharp and he could cut his shirttail off. I told him things were a little different now and since Caleb was now six feet six inches tall and 250 pounds, he could tell him that!

Randy was a tremendous friend whose property provided me with many tremendous turkey hunting memories. It was my great pleasure to take both of my sons, his son, and another young man from church and call in their first turkeys.

Backyard Double

ONE OF THE MANY BLESSINGS in my life has been the friendship of Randy and Susan Wilson and their son, Trent. As I recall, Randy was one of the first people I met after moving to Rockford in Coosa County to assume the position of area biologist on the Coosa Wildlife Management Area.

After getting my bearings in Rockford and after getting married, Melanie and I visited the local Baptist church where Randy and Susan were members. Many studies have indicated that a high percentage of people will come to church if someone would simply ask them. That's what Randy did. I distinctly remember his invitation. When I would see him at the post office or around town he would say, "Come to church." This was not at the end of a conversation; it *was* the conversation. Looking back, I realize it may have been more akin to a command than to an invitation! Whichever was the case, we ended up joining the church and today consider Randy and Susan some of our dearest friends.

Another blessing for me has been that the Wilsons live on a piece of property with an ample population of wildlife. I probably should say they live in among the wildlife. The first deer I killed in Coosa County was shot on their property. The first turkey my oldest son killed was on their property and it was my pleasure to call up the first turkey for their son Trent. I could wax on about the many hunting adventures on the property and as a matter of fact many of the stories in this book are rooted there!

My youngest son, Caleb, and Mr. Randy have been lifelong buddies. I think one of Randy's favorite pastimes was to pester Caleb when he was young. One of his favorite ways to do it was to call Caleb and tell him the turkeys are taking the place over and he needs Caleb to help thin them down. Caleb and I have spent many mornings enjoying hunting the turkeys on the place. While many of the hunts were memorable, one stands out.

We had made a few hunts and knew there were three longbeards staying together on the property. The birds were roosting on a hill almost directly behind the house and after flying down they would walk the edge of the pasture. Saturday morning found me and Caleb waiting on daylight and listening for gobbles. I told Caleb to owl hoot and he was quickly answered by a single gobble. We moved around behind the house and set up against a large pine on the edge of the yard. Seriously, we were sitting within fifty yards of the house when I gave my first call and got a gobble in response. Within a few minutes I saw a gobbler coming around the edge of the pasture. Quickly two more longbeards appeared behind the lead bird. All three of the birds were easing toward us looking for the hen. With my gun lying on the ground beside me, I whispered to Caleb to get his gun on the lead bird. He eased the 20-gauge around as the birds closed the gap between us. With the gobbler at thirty yards I asked Caleb if he had the bead on the bird and did not get a response. I assumed that meant no. A small bush had somehow gotten between Caleb and the bird. The bird took a couple of steps and I saw Caleb snug up against the gun stock. "Do you have it on his neck?" He gave a slight nod and I said, "Shoot him." Now one thing about Caleb is that once he gets the green light to shoot, the shot is on its way! The 20-gauge 870 barked and the lead bird hit the ground. The other two longbeards ran about ten yards, stopped, and came running back and jumped on the bird that had yet to flop. Although I had seen it on video, this was the first time I had ever witnessed such a spectacle. I think Caleb and I were both a little astonished at what was taking place before us. However, Caleb snapped back to himself and yelled, "Shoot one, Dad!" When I say he yelled, he literally shouted it out. Hearing the shout, the two gobblers jumped off the turkey, turned, and looked our way for maybe three seconds and then went right back to flogging the downed bird.

I retrieved my gun and brought it to my shoulder and waited. About twenty seconds later, the gobblers dismounted and separated. I put the bead on one of the birds and pulled the trigger. The bird hit the ground; however, when I jumped up to go toward him, he also jumped up and started running. I fired again and the bird again hit the ground. However, he refused to stay down. A third shot from my 12-gauge brought the gobbler down for good and ended the career of my 12-gauge as my turkey gun!

We gathered the birds and walked the eighty yards to the house where we were met by Randy wearing a grin a mile wide. I had rarely doubled with anyone in the past but during that spring I did it three times. However, the backyard double was a special blessing.

I know of no way to thank the Wilsons for so graciously sharing their blessing with my family and for the blessing they are to us. Thanks again; we love you. Make the time today to thank someone who has been a blessing in your life! You'll be glad you did.

Chasing Homeboy

I COULD NOT BELIEVE my good fortune when I heard the gobbler. I had just returned from listening on two different properties without hearing a turkey. Work, torrential rain, and illness in my family had already fractured my turkey season. You can imagine my elation when I stepped out of my truck and heard the bird open up not three hundred yards from my house. I immediately grabbed my gun and vest and donned my facemask and gloves as I headed toward the bird.

As I neared the natural gas pipeline right-of-way (ROW) that traverses the edge of my property, I realized the bird was just on the other side of the ROW. I dropped down and crawled to an oak tree about twenty feet off the edge of the opening. I hurried to get set up and pulled my worn aluminum Thunderdome call from my vest. As soon as the striker hit the surface the gobbler cut me off. I set the call down and got my gun up. I quickly heard the bird drumming and turned my barrel slightly to the left, where I thought the bird would pop up. He was just below a swale in the field and I anticipated seeing his head any second.

My heart was pumping pretty hard when I heard something that didn't sound like a turkey. I soon realized a vehicle was coming down my driveway which crossed the pipeline about fifty yards from where I thought the bird was currently standing. As the drumming stopped and the vehicle got louder, I held my breath and hoped the vehicle would ease by without totally disrupting the bird.

Suddenly I was no longer feeling very fortunate as the truck's bumper appeared, driving up the pipeline. First my mouth flew open and then the rage ensued. Who on earth would be driving along the pipeline on my property at 8:00 on Saturday morning? As I was reading the decal on the door a second surveyor's truck appeared behind the first. The first truck had passed me and the look on the face of the driver of the second truck showed he wished he had been in the lead instead of being approached by a huge camo blob carrying a shotgun. "I'm sorry" were the first words out of his mouth. Although I never totally lost it, all four members of the surveying crew knew I was not a happy camper. Totally frustrated, I returned to the house.

The next weekend I heard the homeboy gobbler sound off and placed him just south of a food plot on the ROW. I hurried toward him as he continued to gobble. I slid in beside a cherry tree just off the edge of the field and gave a tree yelp that was immediately answered. Homeboy was less than one hundred yards away and a couple of minutes later I saw him pitch off the roost. With him on the ground I offered up my best yelp but got no verbal response. Knowing the gobbler was close I continued to scan with my eyes. Nothing. Although I knew better, the silence was deafening and convinced me to pick up my Thunderdome and try a low yelp. As I set the call down, the gobbler's head and neck appeared at about forty yards. Although I held out hope he had not seen my movement, when he commenced to putting I got the feeling he had. Keeping his eye on me, he began walking and putting with every step. He took about ten steps to his right and then did an about-face and walked back to where he had initially showed up. The whole time I was thinking if he would just duck his head out of sight for a second I would swing on him and shoot when he reappeared. Evidently he knew that old trick. When he did duck his head he was walking straight away and still putting. As a last-ditch effort, I cut on my mouth call and to my surprise the bird double gobbled. Of course that was only to rub it in as he then resumed putting as he widened the difference between us.

Obviously, some of our departmental supervisors do not appreciate the deep need of turkey hunters to be in the woods at daylight during the season. If they did they would refrain from scheduling work opportunities during that time. However, the National Archery in the Schools Program is a very worthy project. The program is enormously popular and we normally have over twelve hundred youth participating in the state championship. Therefore, it is an all-hands-on-deck event. Our major state sponsor is the Alabama chapter of the National Wild Turkey Federation. I guess it was some consolation that members of our state board were also forfeiting a morning of hunting to aid in this worthwhile endeavor.

I had arranged for a couple of coworkers to meet at my house and we would make the hour drive to Montgomery together. As I came out on my porch, my longtime friend and coworker Andy Hughes (another turkey addict) was all excited and asked me, "Did you hear that?" As I listened Homeboy sounded off again. I must admit it was pretty difficult to get in my truck and drive away from the gobbling bird.

The next morning, I was standing in a firebreak about 150 yards from Homeboy's normal roosting spot at daylight. Seeing how his roost tree was within twenty-five yards of the property line and knowing my neighbors were also pursuing him I wanted to be in position to offer him the option of coming my way. I waited for him to fire off but heard nothing. My best owl hoots and crow caws produced nothing at all. Of course whenever that happens my first thought is that somebody got him yesterday.

Work and weather kept me out of the woods for the next few days. However, on Wednesday morning I heard Homeboy sound off as I was leaving. Although it sounded as if he had moved a little to the west, I felt he was still close enough to hunt from the place I had tried him earlier. I vowed, Lord willing, "I'll see you tomorrow."

As I eased into position he gobbled. I thought he had moved almost hundred yards west but would still likely fly down into the pipeline ROW. I gave a tree yelp and he immediately responded. I set my call down and vowed not to pick it back up. When he gobbled again I gave a light yelp on my mouth call. The next thing I heard were wing beats. Remembering his silent approach the last time, I listened close and scanned with my eyes. As I waited as patiently as possible, my neighbor blew on a crow call and Homeboy answered back, revealing he was just left of directly in front of me and about sixty yards out.

As I watched and listened a gobbler head appeared to the right of where I thought the turkey was and about forty-five yards out. The bird was in almost the exact same location as when he had spotted me previously. Trying to control my breathing was a chore as I watched the bird. My neighbor blew the crow call again and a gobble split the early morning air. However, I realized it did not come from the gobbler I was watching but from where I had heard the previous gobble.

Realizing there were two gobblers I began to wonder whether or not the bird I could see was a longbeard or possibly a jake I had thought I had heard on an earlier hunt. Suddenly the gobbler's head dipped out of sight and another appeared about five steps to the east. Unfortunately that was all that appeared: about four inches of head and neck. I did not want to shoot a jake "by mistake," which is easy to do in this type of scenario. However, as I contemplated the situation the neighbor crow called and my question was answered when the bird I was watching hammered back. I judged the distance at forty yards. While I knew the shot was within the capability of my 20-gauge, I also knew that having to shoot through the thick grass in the food plot could disrupt my pattern. As I continued to hold the bead on his head, he continued to answer the crow cawing. Unfortunately, he didn't change his position.

I must admit it is pretty unnerving to have a mature gobbler gobbling and staring a hole through you at forty yards. However, I would much rather he turn and walk away than to try a risky shot and get less than a fatal shot on the monarch of the woods. However, at the time I was sort of at a loss for options.

I had no doubt Homeboy knew exactly where the earlier calls had originated from and I'm sure he was wondering why the ole girl wouldn't step on out. Experience was whispering in my ear that he probably wouldn't stay there much longer. Then an idea finally came to mind.

I decided if I could just scratch in the leaves just a little bit it might lure Homeboy the couple of steps I needed. However, the problem was figuring out how to do the scratching without being spotted. Luckily about four feet in front of me was a large pine tree that was partially hiding my large frame from the probing eyes. With both hands on my gun I raised my right leg ever so slightly and raked my boot across the leaves. This got the bird's attention. He intensified his stare and let out a thunderous gobble. That was followed by what I had hoped for: a step in my direction. I knew better than to wait any longer and I slapped the trigger on the 870. You can imagine what my heart was doing when a gobbler went running to the left and flew. I could only hope it was bird number two as I jumped up and ran into the field. Due to a dip in the terrain I had to run halfway to the bird before I could see him flopping on the ground. I was elated. I looked at my watch and was surprised to see that the episode I thought had lasted an eternity had in fact filled fifteen minutes. Of course anybody who's been there can tell you those minutes of intense staring are much longer than normal minutes!

I stood over the bird and thanked the Creator for making both of us and allowing us to have this interaction. I must admit that while I love turkey hunting, and calling in and killing a gobbler is my goal, I did feel a bit of remorse knowing I wouldn't be able to stand on my porch and hear Homeboy sound off again. However, it was a little easier to take knowing Homeboy Jr. had escaped unscathed and, with a little luck, I might hear him next year. Lord willing, I'll be listening.

Muddy Double

I DON'T KNOW HOW MANY TIMES Blake Kelley and I have hunted turkeys together but suffice it to say it has been a lot. While most hunts are enjoyable, some are more memorable than others. Of course, those when you are successful often seem to stand out.

One April morning found us in the Richville community of Coosa County listening for gobbles. Fortunately, we heard a gobble right off the bat and headed toward the bird. We got as close as we would dare and set up. I offered a series of yelps, which were immediately answered. Over time I have learned that if a bird answers aggressively, I need to offer him the opportunity to come in without me calling too much. As we sat listening, a second bird gobbled pretty far behind us. Things were definitely looking up.

It wasn't long until we heard drumming. I am thankful that I can hear drumming. I have learned that many folks cannot. I think it is a frequency thing. I can hear it; however, I can't hear it as well as Blake can.

Back to the story. While I can hear drumming, determining where it is coming from is another story. Very often it sounds like it is coming from every direction. This was the case this day. Since we had heard two gobblers, it was totally possible that the bird could be either in front of or behind us. I looked at Blake and gave him our sign for drumming, which is tapping my fingers on my leg. He nodded letting me know he had heard the bird. The bird drummed again and I whispered to Blake that I thought it was behind us. Of course, just as those words came out of my mouth I spotted the bird in front of us at about thirty-five yards. I whispered to Blake, "Maybe not."

The bird was to the left of Blake and he was on my left. The bird had us pinned down so we sat motionless, only moving our eyes. It was a cool morning and I think the bird may have spotted our breath. It was obvious it had seen something it didn't like since it straightened up and started walking away. The gobbler was not running but he was picking up the pace. I whispered to Blake that I thought I might could call him back. Just as I said that, Blake quickly raised his single-shot 10-gauge and shot the bird. The gobbler immediately hit the ground and I said, "Well that works too." We jumped up and ran to the bird. It was fifty-two yards to where the gobbler laid motionless. As we were celebrating, the second gobbler sounded off. We quickly gathered up Blake's bird and headed toward gobbler number two.

We moved a couple of hundred yards and solicited another gobble from the bird. I quickly set up where I could shoot down a logging road and Blake sat a few yards behind me. I slipped the straps of my vest off and pulled out my Thunderdome aluminum slate. A couple of yelps received an immediate response. I waited a couple minutes and gave another yelp. The responding gobble let us know the bird had closed the distance. I set the call down. I knew if any more calling was necessary I would use my mouth call.

Within about a minute I spotted the gobbler as he came into the logging road. He was about seventy-five yards down the road but was heading our way. While a logging road often offers a clean shooting lane, it also allows a gobbler to see really well. I was sitting against a tree that was only about eight feet off the side of the road. Fortunately, the bird kept coming without me having to do any more calling. I had picked a spot at about thirty yards where I hoped to shoot the gobbler. When he reached that spot, I pulled the trigger and the bird hit the ground flopping. I jumped to my feet and started toward the bird. However, after the first step I realized there was a problem. It seemed that somehow when I had got to my feet, I had stuck my right foot through the strap of my turkey vest and I was now dragging my vest along behind me. While I was trying to shake the vest loose, the bird was flopping in the muddy logging road. I finally freed my foot and made it to the bird. I could hear Blake laughing hysterically behind me. When I reached the bird, he was totally coated with mud. That was the only time I ever had that happen. I picked up the mud-coated bird and moved it out of the road. Blake came over and I knelt over the bird and thanked the Lord for such a phenomenal morning.

Although my vest and my turkey were totally coated with mud, we were all smiles as we walked out. Although I've killed bigger turkeys, I don't know that any weighed more than my mud-caked trophy! It's a great memory.

Naming Turkeys

EARLY IN MY TURKEY HUNTING CAREER I was anxious to learn all I could about it and therefore read a lot of articles and some books. One thing I ran across more than once was the advice that a hunter should not name a turkey. The thinking was that if you hunt a turkey enough to name it, you will inevitably spend so much time on that bird you likely won't kill any birds. I have found this to be true, yet I've still named a few.

I was so richly blessed by a dear couple of friends that have allowed me to turkey hunt on their property for many years. Randy and Susan Wilson were a couple of the first people I met when I took a wildlife biologist/conservation enforcement officer job in rural Coosa County. After my initial introduction to Randy, each time he would see me he would end the conversation by saying, "Come to church." I took him up on the offer and we have worshiped at Rockford Baptist Church together for the past thirty-six years. Membership in the church has been a true blessing for my family. Seeing how we were over two hundred miles from our nearest relative, it was very beneficial to have a church family. The Lord has said he will never leave us or forsake us. I believe part of that promise is often fulfilled by His hands and feet here on earth: our church family. I can testify that my family has been richly blessed. While I know I would have gone to church somewhere, I've always been thankful for Randy's invite.

I've heard pastors and others say that the major impetus for someone to go to church is that someone invites them! Invite somebody!

Randy and Susan's property was good turkey habitat in that it contained areas of hardwoods, pines, and open fields. Anyone who has hunted an area with large fields knows it can be a challenging place to kill a turkey. If you need to learn the layout of a property, turkey hunting is a good way to do it. I would have to say I know Randy's property as well as any place I've ever hunted. This thorough knowledge often proves to be beneficial when chasing an elusive gobbler. I am often reminded that while I know the place well, the gobblers seem to know it better.

No matter how well someone knows a property, turkeys still have many tools at their disposal to thwart the attempts of those who desire to give them a ride in their turkey vest! I learned this well when I crossed paths with a bad turkey that I eventually named Superglue.

Daylight found me at Randy's listening for gobbles. I heard one and of course he was on the other side of the property. I hurriedly made my way toward the bird. However, by the time I had crossed the creek and climbed the hill the bird had shut up. As always, I stored the location of the bird in my mind to possibly try it the next morning.

On day two the sky began to lighten with me standing within a couple hundred yards of where I thought the bird had been roosted. My first owl hoot was instantly answered and I was feeling pretty good about being able to pinpoint the bird. Now I had to figure out where to try to set up to call the bird in. I skirted the wildlife opening where I thought the bird was likely roosted. Sure enough my next hoot resulted in a loud gobble from the bird, which was probably less than 125 yards away. I decided I was probably close enough so I sat down and tried a tree yelp. The gobbler immediately answered and I knew I was probably in business. I waited for a few minutes and then gave my best fly down cackle. The gobbler immediately blasted it. In my mind's eye, I could see the bird flying down, possibly within gun range, and me carrying him out over my shoulder. Of course, I knew better than to count my chickens before they hatched but hey, a guy can dream.

I waited a few minutes and offered a yelp. The bird responded and I could tell he was still in the tree. I had learned over time that if you call too much to a bird on the roost, it might just decide to sit there. I was beginning to realize this might be that bird. He stayed in the tree until I had to leave. All day my mind kept going back to what I should have done differently.

The next morning, I had a new strategy laid out and couldn't wait to hit the woods. I exited the truck and made my way to the northern boundary of the property. That was the easy part. Climbing the hill and getting set up alongside of the wildlife opening would not be as easy. A lack of any recent rain made moving through the leaves, without sounding like a herd of elephants, a real challenge. As I grew pretty close to where I wanted to be, I was desperately hoping I would not spook the gobbler. As I got to within a few feet of where I wanted to be, I began to wonder whether or not the bird was there or not. I was thinking I had either done a really good job of sliding into place or I had wasted a lot of time going after a bird that wasn't even there.

I slipped the straps of my vest off of my shoulders and removed my slate from my pocket. I used the carbon striker to make a tree yelp that I could barely hear. While it might have been almost silent to me the gobbler sounded off letting me know he had heard it just fine. While this excited me, the fact that he was so close shook me up a little bit. I scoured the trees trying to spot the bird. It's amazing how at times it is so difficult to spot a huge bird sitting in a tree! As I scanned back and forth, I caught the movement of the bird's head as he unleashed another deafening gobble. He was about fifty yards off to my left and he was fired up. I did my best to remain calm, although I couldn't help thinking I was about to put the smack down on this ole boy. Several scenarios were running through my mind. I hoped he would fly down into the wildlife opening, which would likely be in easy range for me to take him. Of course, he could also fly down the hill off the far side of the opening. I debated whether I would stay put or if I should try to get across the open ground while he was under the hill. I knew I would cross that bridge if and when I got to it.

While I felt I was in a good position, I realized I was also pretty much pinned down by the gobbling bird. Even calling to the gobbler was a bit of a risk. I had hunted long enough to know that a gobbler could pinpoint a call to within a ten-foot radius from a quarter of a mile away. Therefore, with me fifty yards from the bird, I was sure he was counting my breaths and the number of times I blinked my eyes!

I offered a quiet yelp and the bird gobbled. However, following the gobble I heard one of the things I had not wanted to hear. It was a yelp on the other side of the opening. The gobbler immediately answered the hen. At that point I decided I probably needed to try to call the hen to me and hopefully the gobbler would want to join the party. I yelped aggressively and got a response from both birds. My thinking was to keep the excitement level up and hopefully the gobbler would pitch down. With the gobbler in the tree and with me now pinpointed, I was only using my mouth call. I again called and both birds responded. I was looking at the gobbler as he pitched out. Unfortunately, he flew directly to the unseen hen. I couldn't feel too dejected having been outdone by the real thing but it was difficult listening to him gobble while she led him away. Tomorrow was another day.

I did not think of much else other than how to get in a better position on the bird. I had developed a plan and hoped the bird would be in the same tree the next morning. I arrived early and put my plan into action. Once again, I was able to slip into the location without spooking the bird I hoped was there. It didn't take long until the morning calm was split by a gobble. I found that once again I was about fifty yards from the roosted bird. He was fired up. With no prompting by me he was sounding off. Eventually I gave a soft yelp that he answered. I watched as the bird walked back and forth on the limb. He responded to my calls but showed no inclination to fly down. This seemed to go on forever. When I eventually looked at my watch, I realized I had been there watching the bird in the tree for two hours! I had tried all I knew to do and none of it had been enough to convince him to fly down.

I heard a low yelp in the distance and the bird immediately gobbled in response. As I watched, a hen eventually came into view down in the hollow. I offered a yelp that was also answered. Shortly thereafter the gobbler flew to the hen. I did my best to agitate the hen and hopefully get her to come my way with the gobbler in tow but once again it was not to be. I watched as she led the ole boy away.

I could continue to tell you how the same thing happened for several days. I decided I had to name that turkey Superglue since on multiple days I watched him stay glued in the tree until a hen came into view and only then would he fly down. While it was extremely aggravating for me, it was a strategy that worked well for the bird. He survived the entire season! And the next one!

I did not keep count, but on several mornings, I sat and watched Superglue as he gobbled in the tree until a hen would come to him. On the days a hen did not show up, he would gobble at what I offered but it was like he was glued in the tree. The next season, Superglue did not roost in the same tree or area. I do not know what might have happened to him. While I enjoyed hunting him, it did get pretty frustrating.

When telling this story, I've had more than one person state they would have either crawled up under the tree in the dark and shot him off of the limb or killed him with a .22 rifle. There justification was he was probably keeping several other turkeys shut down. When I was told this, I did not react positively. In my book, anyone who would shoot a turkey off of a limb or with a rifle because they could not call him in does not deserve to call themselves a turkey hunter. That's definitely not what I would call them. For me, it's about the hunt. Taking the bird is just gravy.

Wait Until They Are Close Enough

I **HAVE ENJOYED INTRODUCING FOLKS** to turkey hunting. However, it doesn't come without some frustration. Of course, anyone who has turkey hunted very much knows some stuff is just going to happen when you turkey hunt. Sometimes turkeys act as if they don't even want you to kill them! They often do not act as they should. You never know just what might happen and that is true if you are talking about the turkeys or the hunters!

I once had permission to hunt turkeys on a property south of Rockford. It was a somewhat narrow piece of land; however, it did hold several birds from time to time. I remember one morning when I experienced what I hear the TV hunters call a flash hunt. I was walking down the one logging road that led into the property. I had walked about fifty yards from my truck, which was parked near the dirt county road. I owl hooted and a gobbler nearly blew my hat off. He was so close I did not know whether or not I could make it to an oak tree on the right side of the road about fifteen steps ahead of me. A quick glance around the area told me I had to either get to the tree or just sit down in the middle of the road. I stealthily tiptoed to the tree.

I had my Perfection Piggy Back mouth call in my mouth. It had sounded like the bird was roosted right over the logging road. I settled my gun on my knee and gave a very low yelp.

I immediately heard a wing beat and saw the gobbler flying down into the road. He hit the ground and ran straight to me and I shot him at about twenty-five steps. To the best of my memory it is the fastest hunt I have ever experienced. I thanked the Lord for the successful hunt and made the short walk to my truck. I knew where my hunting buddy, Blake, was hunting and I drove by and left a breast feather under his windshield wiper!

Another day found me on the same property; however, this time I had my uncle Reed in tow. We got out of the truck and heard a distant turkey gobble. Unfortunately, the turkey was across the county road and pretty deep in a property where we did not have permission to hunt. I told Uncle Reed there was always the chance we could call the bird across the road. I explained to him that although the dirt county road didn't get much traffic, we would have to be 100 yards off the road to be legal. This was before the legislature messed up our hunting-from-the-road law. Don't get me started.

We gathered our gear and headed down the logging road away from the gobbling bird. We had gone about 150 yards when the turkey gobbled again. I told Uncle Reed that was either a different turkey or the bird had moved toward us. We went a little farther and I found a place for us to set up and call from.

I started with a loud aggressive yelp that received an immediate answer. That was good; however, I told Uncle Reed that if I wasn't mistaken I thought I heard two turkeys gobble. I called again and sure enough there were two gobblers answering. I could tell one of the birds was deeper in the woods than the other. It took a considerable amount of coaxing but eventually the birds began moving our way.

As I listened to the birds, I could tell the farthest bird was closing the distance between them. I told Uncle Reed that if we were really lucky we might could call both birds in. Uncle Reed had only been turkey hunting for a couple of years and had not experienced having two birds come in. Of course, I had only had it happen a time or two myself.

Eventually it was evident the birds had gotten together. My calls were regularly receiving multiple gobbles and it wasn't that long until I spotted the two birds. This was something I had never seen before or since. The two gobblers were strutting in the middle of the county road!

I told Reed I had never had that happen before. About that time, I heard a noise and realized it was a car coming down the road. Knowing the birds would have to go one way or the other, I began aggressively calling in hopes they would come our way. As the vehicle got closer, the birds folded up and ran our way. I told Uncle Reed to get ready.

This is one thing that has often been a point of contention between me and new hunters. To me, being ready when set up on a turkey means you have your gun against your shoulder and pointed in the direction you think the turkey is going to come from. Having your gun in your lap is *not* ready. Many times, I've explained to new hunters if they wait to raise their gun a turkey will often catch the movement and will be in the next county before you can get a bead on him. You definitely want as little movement as possible when a gobbler is within gun range. Even with as little movement as it takes to slide my safety off, I've had gobblers catch it. I've heard old turkey hunters claim that a gobbler can see you bat your eye from twenty yards away. I don't know if that is true, but I can tell you a hunter had better act as if it's true!

The birds were coming our way and I told Uncle Reed to get ready. I also told him to wait until both birds got within range and for him to shoot the one on the left and I would shoot the one on the right. I had yelped lightly and the birds were walking our way. Unfortunately, the lead bird was about fifteen yards in front of the second bird. I hoped Uncle Reed would wait until the second bird was in range before he shot. About the time I thought that thought, *BOOM*. The lead bird hit the ground flopping and the second bird ran for the hills. I jumped up and ran to the bird and placed my foot on its neck. It was a good turkey. Uncle Reed was all smiles when he walked up and then he said, "Why didn't you shoot the other one?" I then explained the one he had shot was barely in range and the other one was fifteen yards farther out. He said he thought they were both close enough. While I would have liked to have doubled on the birds, it was a great hunt. A memory I cherish. Hey, at least he had his gun up and ready!

That's Why They Call Them Turkeys

MY YOUNGEST SON is still in the age group where he thinks I am old as dirt and don't have a clue. Well he has a point; however, I hope one day he will understand I was a little smarter than he thought.

One area where we differ greatly is music. No, he isn't into head-banging crazy noise; however, he is into modern-day artists. Don't get me wrong; he was raised on seventies music and still has the Eagles, Lynyrd Skynyrd, and Bob Seger on his playlist. However, it also contains a lot of new artists. Recently we were in the car and he assumed control of the audio as he often does. I usually tune out or insert my earphones. However, I happened to be listening as a song titled "Old Friends" came on. I listened to the words and tears came to my eyes. The gist of the song is you can't make old friends. There is a lot of truth to that.

During the turkey season I received a call from an old friend from graduate school. We had spoken months earlier and had vowed to get together for a turkey hunt this season. He asked if we could schedule a hunt. I told him we would definitely make it happen.

Phil and I met at Mississippi State University when we were both pursuing our master's degrees in wildlife ecology. Phil quickly became a close friend. After I had graduated and began work as a wildlife biologist for Alabama Game and Fish, I invited Phil to come to Coosa County for a turkey hunt. On that hunt, we called in and killed my first turkey. It was a great hunt. I shot the adult bird at thirty-eight yards. I immediately jumped up and ran to the bird. It was a fine gobbler weighing in at nineteen pounds with a nine-and-a-half-inch beard and not a sign of a spur on either leg! I admit I felt a little cheated. However, that began a love affair with the wild turkey, which I still enjoy.

With the date of our hunt set, I decided we would hunt on my uncle's forty-four-acre parcel of land. Any turkey hunter knows a tract that size limits your options. However, I had enjoyed some great hunts there the past year.

Just prior to the turkey season, a close friend asked if I would take his fourteen-year-old grandson, Hogan, turkey hunting. I was happy to oblige. I contacted the young man and went to his house and gave him and his ten-year-old brother a crash course in Turkey 101. We discussed camouflage, setup, turkey eyesight, gun handling, and shot placement. The next morning, we were on the property of a good friend listening for gobbles. We were fortunate to hear a bird and we hurried to get into position. I was coaching the entire time. The bird gobbled fairly well and was soon headed our way. I told Hogan to watch for what looked like a baseball moving through the woods.

The woods were wide open and I spotted the bird when he was about one hundred yards out. I whispered to Hogan to turn to his right and that I could see the turkey. He made the move and was scanning for the turkey when he excitedly exclaimed, "I see it!" I told him to keep quiet and to take his safety off. He again excitedly said, "There's two of them!" I told him to keep his eye on the front one.

The bird had reached a logging road and was on course for a good shot. When the bird was directly below us I scratched in the leaves behind my back and he stopped. I asked Hogan if he had the sight on the bird's neck and he said he did. I said, "Shoot him." He yanked the trigger; however, the gun did not go off. I knew the safety was off and I knew he had pulled on what he thought was the trigger; however, nothing happened except that the turkey extended his neck and was now staring a hole through us. I again asked if he had the bead on the gobbler's neck and he said yes. I again said, "Shoot him." He pulled the trigger and I saw the bird hit the ground. Hogan, however, did not see it because he was turned around looking at me and asking whether or not he had hit it. As I was getting to my feet I told him he did and I took off down the hill to the bird.

It was a tremendous first gobbler weighing in at eighteen pounds with a ten-inch beard and one-inch spurs. We knelt over the bird and thanked the Lord for His creation and for blessing us with such an awesome experience. As you can imagine, he was hooked!

With the date of my hunt with Phil coming up, I decided to go to the property and check things out. Hogan had texted me and asked if I would take him hunting on Friday. I told him I would. We eventually heard two gobblers. We set up on the closest bird but could not get him to cooperate. The other bird was across the creek and off the property. I told him we would go toward him and see if we could get him interested. As we approached the creek I explained how it was often difficult to get a bird to cross a creek. I called to the bird and he enthusiastically answered. I told Hogan we would set up and see what happened.

I set Hogan up at what looked like a good spot and told him I needed to tend to a call of nature and would be back shortly. As I was finishing the "paperwork," I heard Hogan scratching on his slate call. The bird answered and I could tell he had cut the distance in half! I hurried back and sat down with Hogan and pointed out where I thought the bird would come in. I called again and the bird hammered it. I told Hogan to turn to his right and watch the road because the bird would be there shortly. Within a minute I saw the bird in the road and told my partner to get the gun to his shoulder. The bird was steadily walking toward us until he wasn't. At thirty-five yards he abruptly stopped. I did not know what the problem was but there obviously was one. Unfortunately, some debris between Hogan and the bird prevented a shot. The bird turned and began walking off to our right. He did not putt but was obviously leaving. The bird walked away and I sat there trying to figure out what had happened.

I told Hogan the turkey obviously saw something he did not like but I had no idea what it was. Hogan said, "That's why they call them turkeys." We were both in full camo with face masks and gloves. As I pondered the situation, Hogan said, "He may have saw my boot." I looked at his boot, which was a brown leather cowboy type boot, and I said I didn't think that would have scared the bird. He then said, "They are red on the bottom." He turned his foot around and sure enough the sole of the boot had bright-red soles. I told him to sit still and I moved to the spot where the gobbler had been and sure enough the red boot sole was shining like a stop sign. And that was just the effect it had! Had I known the boots were red on the bottom, I definitely would have had him wear something else from a safety standpoint. Who looks at the bottom of someone's boots?

Knowing there were a couple of gobblers there, Phil and I went back to the property two days later. The gobbler was in the same tree he had been in previously. We were soon set up about seventy-five yards from the gobbling bird. Phil was set up about twenty-five feet in front of me and toward the bird. I called sparingly and the bird answered everything I did. Some of the calls were so quiet I wasn't sure Phil could hear them; however, the gobbler did and responded with lusty gobbles. Finally, after about forty-five minutes of gobbling in the tree, we saw the bird fly down. With him on the ground, I gave a few aggressive yelps. I immediately heard the bird drumming. I got my gun to my shoulder and waited for the bird to appear. Phil was ready as well. We both kept scanning for the gobbler we knew would soon come into view. We kept scanning and waiting. And waiting. I eventually gave another call that was immediately followed by silence. After a few minutes I crawled over to Phil and asked him what happened. He replied he had seen the bird fly down and that was it.

I tried some loud calling that I hoped would get the bird to sound off. We had also heard a distant second bird that I hoped might answer. Evidently both of the bird's shifts had ended as we did not hear another turkey sound.

As we gathered our gear and started walking out, I looked at my gobble counter and saw I had recorded sixty-five gobbles from the two birds. We discussed what had taken place and really couldn't come up with anything we should have done differently. Although we were a little disappointed that the bird did not come in, we agreed it was a great hunt nonetheless. When we made it back to the truck, I said to Phil, "Let me check the soles of your boots!"

Many years ago, I wrote an article titled "The Best Worst Season I Ever Had." It was the season when I did not kill a bird but called up turkeys for my two sons. This season reminded me of that one. Good times in the turkey woods spent with new friends, old friends, and loved ones. That's hard to beat, even if the turkeys act like turkeys!

Troublesome Bait

LET ME BEGIN THIS STORY with an admission. I'm addicted to turkey hunting. That's the only way I can explain getting up an hour before daylight forty-five days in a row and going and standing in the woods and hooting like an owl. Those who haven't tried it probably have a difficult time understanding it. Turkey hunting is matching wits with an ultra-paranoid bird that can see a gnat at a hundred yards and pinpoint a field mouse fart farther than that. He knows every tree on his home turf and often can spot an interloper for a country mile! Pursuing a gobbler is often a woodland chess match. Calling in and taking a wild turkey can be one of the most exciting experiences one may ever experience. Yes, I'm hooked.

Having this passion for the monarch of the woods, you can understand why I would hold utter disdain for anyone who would attempt to take one of the birds illegally. Not only does that go against my sense of ethics it may also often cost me a morning in the woods chasing turkeys. I can't put up with that.

For me, one of the lowest of the low is the person who will shoot a turkey over a baited area. Unfortunately, often during the early part of the turkey season there is a lack of food for turkeys in the woods. Therefore, some scattered corn or wheat will easily bring the birds in. This is unfair and unhealthy for the birds. This is especially true now in that many folks will purchase what is labeled as deer corn and put it out for turkeys. Unfortunately, "deer corn" is often labeled as such since it contains enough impurities that it cannot be sold for consumption by livestock. This corn often carries a high level of aflatoxin, which can be fatal to turkeys and other wildlife. Of course, the folks who will shoot a turkey over bait aren't concerned with the health of wildlife. It burns me up. Unfortunately, there has been a close correlation of feeding/baiting of wildlife and an increase in disease in wildlife. It's just a bad idea.

As you have gathered, I hold anyone who would hunt turkeys over bait in low esteem. However, some are worse than others. Individuals who will bait on public land have no regard for wildlife or for anyone else hunting on the property. I have experienced this type of activity a few times on the Coosa Wildlife Management Area (WMA). To the best of my knowledge, Coosa has had a good turkey population since it began allowing turkey hunting, which was around sixty years ago. Coosa is one of the few counties in the state that never had any turkey restocking take place. This was due in part to the population of turkeys on the WMA. Even after a tremendous amount of the hardwood on the area was cut and replaced by loblolly pine, the turkey population remained strong. Of course, I believe another reason that helped the birds to survive on the area was the treacherous terrain they liked to inhabit.

Back in its heyday, the area would have hunters from as many as twelve or thirteen states in the campground during the spring turkey season. I normally enjoyed stopping by the campground and talking with the hunters. Hunting was only allowed until 1:00 in the afternoon so you could usually find many of the hunters in the campground in the afternoon. Just like deer hunters, the turkey hunters were always asking where the best place would be to find a gobbling bird. At that time the WMA was thirty-eight thousand acres in size and the majority of it was good habitat. Therefore, it was fairly easy to give them a recommendation. I once had a couple of fellows from West Virginia in the campground. When they asked where they should go, I told them I had seen some birds on the northwest side of the area. They asked how far it was from our current location and I told them it was about three miles as the crow flies. I told them I could give him driving directions if they wanted me to. One of the guys said if I would mark the area on their map, they would just walk there. I marked the area but then told the guy there was some treacherous terrain between where we were and where I was talking about. He scoffed at that and said he climbed bigger hills than these going to his mailbox. I told him to knock himself out.

A couple days later, I again stopped by and spotted the guys in the campground. The fellow who had not made the comment told me to ask the other one how he had enjoyed his hike. I asked how it had gone and he said the fellow had left the campground an hour before daylight and did not make it to the marked area until nearly four hours later. I thought if checking his mail was worse than that he probably hates having to check his mail!

What was it I was talking about? Oh yeah, public land baiters. I've already explained why baiting is a bad idea; however, baiting on public land is even worse due to the high probability that someone who had not baited the area could easily be caught hunting over it. You can imagine how you would feel being accused of such a thing when you were in fact innocent of it. Therefore, bait on a public area required me to put forth a lot of effort to be sure I apprehended the proper ne'er-do-well.

One spring many years ago I received information an area of the WMA was baited. The informant said he had inadvertently walked into the area that had been baited with wheat. He provided some good directions, which was imperative when you were talking about a thirty-eight-thousand-acre area with two hundred miles of roads. The area was on the north side of the property not far from one of the two campgrounds that were on the WMA at the time.

Since all hunters had to be out of the woods by 1:00 p.m., I waited until the afternoon to try and find the illegal site. I followed the good directions and located a spot where someone had obviously parked a vehicle several times. I parked in the same spot. The area was in a somewhat narrow hardwood drain. It did not take long to locate the telltale scratched up area that results when a group of turkeys are searching for food. I surveyed the area and located where the fellow had been sitting. Unlike most folks who baited an area, this individual had not built a blind per se to help conceal him from the sharp-eyed birds. However, he had cut a few canes and had stuck them in the ground. This gave a little concealment but did not hinder his ability to shoot. The violator had been sitting against a large oak tree that was only about twenty yards from the baited area.

I mentioned earlier that a turkey possesses a tremendous sense of sight. I have heard many people say that if a turkey could smell you would never be able to kill one of them. That might be true. Obviously, this individual did not think a turkey could smell very well based on the numerous cigarette butts stuck into the dirt around the base of the tree. I retrieved a sample of the wheat that was being used as bait and I also collected one of the cigarette butts and hurried out of the area.

I decided it would be best to catch the fellow sitting in the bait and that would mean I would probably go in a couple of hours after daylight. I hope you are wondering why I would not go in immediately after daylight. Well there is a good reason for that. Having worked several turkey baiting cases, I learned that many folks with a propensity to hunt over bait will listen for a gobbler and attempt to call one up at first light. If they do not hear a turkey or are unsuccessful in calling one in, they will then move to their baited area and sit there for a few hours. Of course, some folks will go straight to the bait to begin with. Waiting to go in on someone can be problematic since you never really know what time they will decide to leave the area. It is tricky sometimes.

As a general rule on the WMA folks who were hunting legitimately would normally have a starting point where they would listen for gobbles. If they heard one, they would take off toward the bird in an effort to get to it before all the other folks that also heard that bird. This is where a thorough knowledge of the WMA road system could definitely be a benefit. After the initial gobbling was over, some folks would sit in the woods and call for a while, while others would ride around on the area. During this time, I would often set up a roadblock and check hunters. Thinking about working the bait, I was trying to decide whether or not to try and check some moving hunters or to just go to the bait. As was often the case, I decided just to play things by ear and see what the day provided.

I arrived at the WMA shop around 7:00 a.m. We tried not to do too much roadwork or tractor work too early during the turkey season as not to disturb hunters on the area. At the shop I fueled and serviced some equipment while I was waiting on folks to start moving. About 8:00 a.m. I got in my truck and started driving across the area. I decided I would just check folks as I encountered them instead of setting up in any one area. While I saw a few vehicles parked along the underwater bridge road, traffic was light and I only saw a couple of vehicles that were moving.

I crossed the underwater bridge and headed up toward what we referred to as the ridge road. The ridge road traversed the entire WMA on the north side. If my memory serves, the road was about eleven miles long with about seven or eight major roads feeding off of it. It was a good place to find some folks. However, I decided to head on toward the baited spot and at least see if there were any vehicles in the area. I turned toward the Dickson Park campground and took the side road that led to the bait.

I was just easing along the road when I spotted a pickup truck parked in the spot where I had parked when looking for the bait. I pulled up behind the truck and noticed it had a Talladega County tag. I slipped out of my truck and took a good look around. The only thing I spotted was a cigarette butt next to the door of the truck. It matched the one I had collected earlier. I decided to head on toward the bait.

I had mentally laid out a route that would hopefully keep my approach concealed as well as bring me in behind where I thought the violator would be. You did not want to walk straight into where the poacher was looking for several reasons. If you approached in front of them, they might see you and take off running. More importantly that approach would also mean you were likely walking straight into where their weapon was pointed. I did not want to do that. However, experience had told me there were no guarantees as to where they would be or which way they might be facing. Keep in mind, my culprit would also be in full camouflage. You had to move slow and constantly search the area with your eyes.

In this case, I quickly learned that most of my preparation was for naught seeing how as I started toward the bait I spotted a camo-clad fellow walking up out of the drain. I slid in beside a tree and waited on the man to come to me. Yes, I would have rather caught him sitting watching the bait; however, I had learned a while back that you had to be able to roll with the punches. As I watched the man approaching my location, I was running through the questioning I would need to use to make this case. As always, I was cognizant of the fact that I did not want to startle this guy and have him send a load of #4 shot my way.

When the fellow was about sixty feet away and behind a couple of trees I utilized my tried-and-true method of revealing myself. I whistled. Someone whistling isn't a common sound in the woods and it normally does a good job of letting someone know there is someone else in the woods without startling them. The man came to an abrupt stop. I called out, "State game warden." From my covered location, I told the man to go ahead and unload his shotgun. He quickly shucked three shells out onto the ground. When he reached down to retrieve the shells I moved toward his location. I asked if he was having any luck and he replied he had not heard anything. I asked if the nearby gray Chevrolet pickup was his and he advised it was. I told him we could walk up to his truck and once there I would like to take a look at his license and permit.

We made our way out to the road and back to the trucks. He opened the door of his truck and laid his shotgun in the seat. As he began fishing out his hunting license and WMA permit I asked if he had any other weapons on him or in his vehicle. He immediately told me he did not. I told him I was going to check. The vehicle was one of the first extended-cab trucks that were manufactured. It did not have a third door, only a little extra room behind the seat. I looked in the truck and behind the seat where I saw something significant; however, I did not let on. I looked under the seat and there found an old .38-caliber pistol. When I say old, I mean old. I think the date on the barrel was 1940 something. It was the first pistol I had ever seen that broke open in the middle. It took me a minute to figure it out but when I did unhinge it I found it was fully loaded. It was a WMA violation to possess the pistol and to have it loaded in the vehicle. The man said he had forgotten the pistol was in the truck. I carried it and put it in my truck.

I returned to the man and took his license and permit and examined them and returned them to him. While I had considered some preliminary questions, I decided to cut to the chase. I informed the man that the area where he was hunting was baited and intently watched and listened for his response. He tried to look totally startled but I could tell his heart wasn't in it. However, he did not say anything. That was interesting in that most folks would immediately start claiming they did not know the area was baited and that if it was they didn't have anything to do with it. I just held my gaze and waited for him to say something. He didn't. Which to me said a lot.

We were in an interesting position in that he did not deny the area was baited while at the same time he did not acknowledge the area was baited. While we could have kept playing the cat-and-mouse game, I decided to again cut to the chase. I asked the fellow what he thought a judge would say if I told him the cigarette butts I found at the bait site matched the one I found beside his truck and the ones I was sure were in his pocket. He thought for a minute and with a bit of a grin replied, "A lot of people smoke." While I didn't think that was much of a defense, I admitted that was true. I then quickly asked, "How many folks do you think smoke this same brand of cigarettes and have a bag of wheat in the back floorboard of their truck?" The grin immediately left his face but quickly returned and he said, "You got me."

I issued the man a ticket for hunting by the aid of bait and for having a loaded gun in a vehicle. I explained the area would be considered baited for ten days after all the bait was gone. He stated he understood and he would not be back. He signed his tickets and got in his truck and drove away.

The cases were called in the next district court and the man approached the bench and pled guilty to both charges.

What about you? Do you know what it feels like to be caught? Not that good of a feeling. We all probably know that feeling. It's a sinking feeling when you know you are caught and are about to have to pay the price. Well we are all in that boat. We all make mistakes. We all sin. The Bible says the wages of sin is death. We will all die. However, there is a second part to the verse that says all have sinned and come short of the glory of God. The next line says but the gift of God is eternal life through Jesus Christ. There is only One who can forgive our sins and promise us eternal life. Choose Jesus!

The Best Worst Season
I Ever Had

JUST STAY CALM. Those were the words I whispered to the twelve-year-old to my right and the thirteen-year-old directly in front of me. Whether the words were spoken for their benefit or mine I wasn't really sure. "He's going to pop up right on those rocks," I whispered. To me, the drumming was deafening; however, I wasn't certain whether or not the two young hunters even heard it. "Get your gun ready," I whispered. I would find myself saying that a lot during the best worst season I ever had.

An old turkey hunting adage in my neck of the woods says that skinny turkeys don't gobble. As the Alabama spring turkey season got into full swing I was beginning to believe that the poor mast crop the year before was taking its toll on the gobbling activity. Although a bird would gobble well occasionally, it was the exception to the rule. After many very uneventful mornings, it didn't take long for my ears to perk up when a young man at my church mentioned all of the turkeys he was seeing at his house. I was quick to tell him that whenever he wanted to chase a gobbler to give me a call. Although I didn't sit by the phone, I was glad when the call came.

I have known Trent Wilson literally all of his life. He and my twelve-year-old son, Justin, were friends growing up. Although

Trent had several deer to his credit, I knew he had yet to take a turkey and I was excited about possibly making it happen. We set a day and Justin and I arrived at 5:00 a.m. Trent met us and said he had heard a turkey a couple of days before on the ridge behind the house. I said that sounded like a good place to start if we could hear over the noise of the cows. Unfortunately for us, Trent and his dad had separated the cows from the calves the previous evening and neither the mommas nor the babies liked it one bit. As we eased down the road with the cows following us and bellowing as loudly as they could, my hopes were fading.

At 5:15 a.m. I caught a break in the noise and gave an owl hoot that was followed immediately by a gobble. That made me feel a lot better; however, the fact that the gobbler was on the very top of the ridge with a good 360-degree view didn't excite me. I quickly decided that going straight at this bird would not work and I developed a plan of attack. I told the boys that in order to get up on the ridge with the bird, we would have to go down the hollow and then try to work our way back to him. We hurriedly made our way down the hollow until I thought we were far enough past the bird that we could safely ease up on the ridge. I cautioned both boys to move slowly and quietly. I started up the hill and immediately had a turkey fly off the ridge over our heads. I told the boys that I didn't think it was our bird that had flown out and we continued moving up the hill. After moving about sixty yards, it became obvious that we still couldn't get on top of the ridge without a good chance of spooking the gobbler. As I was trying to decide our next move, I spotted a hen, which in turn spotted us. I told the boys to sit down while I thought about my next move. The hen putted a few times but wasn't really sure if we posed a threat or not. I knew that a hen sitting above us putting probably wouldn't really increase our chances so I made the decision to try to spook the hen into leaving.

It didn't take a lot of encouragement to get the hen to leave; however, when she flew out, another turkey beyond her flew out as well and it was a big one. I sat down and told the boys that I might have just messed us up and I would try to solicit another gobble. Fortunately, my hoot was answered by a gobble. Unfortunately, the bird was now on the ground. I quickly moved the boys up the hill as far as I thought I could. It had been a long time since I had hunted with two other people and I had forgotten how difficult it was. We were soon settling in on the side of the ridge. I estimated some distances and pointed out to Trent how far he could shoot. I then gave a series of soft yelps that was immediately answered by a gobble. I quickly turned Trent toward where the gobble came from and had him get his gun ready. A gobble and then running in the leaves followed my next yelp. I whispered to Trent that the turkey was coming and he would probably pop up on a rocky outcropping slightly above us.

The drumming was having its usual effect on me. The hair on my neck was standing up and I could feel my pulse and hear my breathing. I noticed that Trent's breathing had picked up a little also. I softly told him to be ready and then I lightly scratched in the leaves. That was all it took and a huge gobbler in full strut emerged on the rocks. Then another stepped up on his right and then another on his left. We were fortunate they didn't see my mouth, which had fallen open! I whispered to Trent to get on the middle bird and when he stuck his head up to shoot him. I gave a light cluck and the head came up and Trent blew him down. The other two gobblers stood and looked at the bird lying still on the ground. Although I had my gun in my hand and it instinctively started up, I quickly realized this was Trent's moment and I laid my gun down and jumped up and ran toward the bird. I told Trent to put his safety on as I quickly covered the twenty-four steps to where the bird lay motionless.

I could see the broad smiles through their camo masks as the boys hurried to the bird. After the slapping on the back was completed, we knelt over the bird and thanked the Lord for letting us enjoy His creation. Trent then slung the bird over his shoulder and headed toward the house. It was then that I realized that the bird not only had a nine-and-a-half-inch beard, but it also had two other beards. The beard above the long beard measured three and a half inches and the one above it measured one inch. The trek to the house through the bellowing cows didn't take long and we were soon in the middle of an intense photo session.

Trent's success kindled Justin's desire to try his hand behind the gun and the next week found me once again leading the juvenile train through the woods chasing a distant gobble. Our morning had begun well enough with a gobbler sounding off at daybreak. Unfortunately, he shut up about as quickly as he started. I knew the area where the gobbler was and eased in and tried some light yelping. It seemed obvious the birds did not want to cooperate so I got the caravan up and moving once again. We moved another hundred yards and paused to listen. Immediately I heard drumming and began trying to get the boys into position. With one boy against a six-inch oak and the other in front of a dogwood, I hunkered down behind them and gave a soft yelp. Once again, I could hear the gobbler drumming and finally decided he was in the hollow below us. I listened as the drumming continued to move to our left until I could no longer hear it. Yelps, clucks, and cutting produced nothing.

After about fifteen minutes of silence my two young partners were ready to move on. I had them stand up and told them to listen as I tried some aggressive yelps. The yelps were answered; however, the gobbler was in the total opposite direction than where the drumming bird had been. In addition, I had a sinking feeling that the bird was across a major creek. We started making our way toward the bird and were quickly in the creek bottom. I asked Trent if their property went across the creek and he assured me that it did. Every yelp would bring a strong gobble in response. I quickly assessed the situation and decided our best bet would be to get as close to the creek bank as possible. I hustled the boys across the bottom and sat down at the base of the largest tree available. I sat with Justin on my right and Trent on his right. I told the boys we would need to let the gobbler get as close to the bank as possible before we tried a shot. I yelped and the gobbler responded from what sounded like maybe 150 yards. Soon I spotted the bird as he made his way to us. I asked if the boys saw him and Trent replied yes and Justin no. The bird came as if he were tied to a string. I told the boys to get their guns ready and wait until the bird was on the bank.

At this point, the bird was coming so well I thought he might fly across the creek, which now would be the worst possible thing since we were so close to the bank he would no doubt land behind us. I held my breath as the bird continued walking straight at our setup. The gobbler didn't break stride until he was within five steps of the creek. He then hopped up on the bank and looked straight at the three camo-clad lumps sitting against the tree. Our setup was good, but it wasn't that good. I was begging the boys to shoot as the bird craned his neck for a better look. The longbeard decided he had seen enough. Just as he turned 180 degrees, I raised my gun to my shoulder and was then rocked as Justin fired on the bird. The bird immediately disappeared into a small depression and I covered him with my gun while telling the boys to check the safety on their guns. I saw the wings flapping and told Justin he had just harvested his first bird. I embraced my son and told him I loved him and was glad we were able to share the experience. Retrieving the bird turned out to be quite a chore, although we didn't seem to mind.

I finished my season by calling in two longbeards, one of which was taken by my uncle, and then by passing a gobbler that I could not identify as such while he was in range. I hate it when that happens! Therefore, I ended the season without harvesting a gobbler. In that sense, it was the worst season I ever had. However, on the other hand, I called in gobblers for two young men who had never harvested a bird. I called in a longbeard for my uncle (his second ever) and I spent numerous days afield pursuing the elusive monarch of the woods. You know, I think this was the best worst season I've ever had. I hoped next year would be this bad!

Exclusive Hunting Rights

HUNTING RIGHTS FOR TURKEYS is a precious commodity in Alabama. I find it interesting when I watch some of the game warden shows on television. Often at the end of the show they give a synopsis of what happened to the folks whose apprehension was depicted on the episode. It is interesting for me to see the fines that were levied against the violators. As I watched the follow-up roll across the screen, I was shocked when it revealed the fine for hunting without permission was $135. While I understand there are many different charges and a wide range of fines, I couldn't help but think they didn't want to try that in Alabama. Our minimum fine for hunting without a permit is $1,000 for a first offense. We play hardball!

I have been blessed with having multiple spots of private property to pursue the monarch of the woods. However, I have found that my pattern is often to stay after a gobbling turkey until either I get him or he makes it obvious that I won't!

Many years ago, Blake Kelley and I were hunting a property in the central part of the county that held several birds. We had enjoyed some success and were trying to get a bird that had been a challenge. We made our way onto the property before daylight and were slowly walking toward where we had heard the bird on previous days.

We had reached a good listening spot and I asked Blake to offer a hoot. The call was not answered by a gobble but did receive some attention. In just a minute we observed someone coming down the road toward us at a fast pace. The man basically ran up to us and in a not-so-nice tone proclaimed he had the exclusive hunting rights on the property and we were trespassing. I wasn't exactly sure how to answer that seeing how we had permission to be on the property and I wasn't sure that he did. I asked his name and he told me who he was. His attitude was belligerent to say the least. Although his face was covered by his face mask, I could tell Blake was none too happy with the fellow.

The man carried on with his tirade and ended it by saying we had parked right under where the turkey normally roosted. We did not see the need to tell the fellow we had taken that bird the day before. I told the man we hoped we had not messed him up too badly and hoped he had some luck. As we walked out Blake asked me who the guy was. I told him I had heard his name before but wasn't sure who he was. I said I would contact the landowner and see what was up. Blake then commented that it was all he could do not to slug the guy when he was being so belligerent.

That afternoon I received a phone call from the property owner, who was fit to be tied. He asked if I had encountered the man on the property that morning and I told him I had. He was mad as a hornet and apologized to me for the incident. I told him it wasn't a problem and he replied that yes it was. He explained what had occurred. It seemed a wealthy landowner had donated a hunt to be auctioned and some folks had paid a high price for it. Unfortunately, they had gone to the man's property but could not hear a bird there. Therefore, the man's assistant had called the home of the landowner where I had been hunting to see if he could take the people to his property to try to hear a bird. The man had spoken with the landowner's wife, who had said as far as she knew it would be okay for him to go to the property and that was how he had ended up there. The landowner again apologized to me and assured me it would never happen again. I told him it was not a problem and I had other places to go. The man then asked me if I had a motorcycle. I definitely had not anticipated that question and wasn't sure what it had to do with anything but I told him I did. He said he would like for me to take the motorcycle to his property the next morning and ride up and down every hill over there. He went on to say the fellow who had called his wife was a leech on the wealthy man's rear end and he didn't want him to hear anything but my motorcycle the next morning. I told him I would not be able to do that. I enjoyed many great turkey mornings on that property but I must admit that was one of the most memorable!

A Season Like No Other in More Ways Than One

WHO KNEW THE 2020 TURKEY SEASON would be totally encapsulated in a worldwide pandemic. The pandemic impacted much of my life but, thankfully, turkey hunting not so much! Although there was a stay-at-home order in effect, when you are addicted to turkey hunting, as I am, it was an essential activity.

Although I love sharing turkey hunting with others and had a couple of tremendous shared hunts during the previous season, turkey hunting is often an individual pursuit. I wish I had filmed each hunt of the season because telling you about them doesn't do them justice. However, I will share one of the most unbelievable hunts I have ever had. It's all true, I promise.

The title says it was a season like no other in more ways than one and that is so true.

Once the turkey season is in I have little need for an alarm clock. The anticipation of the hunt wakes me prior to the alarm sounding. The morning of April 18 I woke up at 5:00 a.m. I knew the forecast had called for rain in the morning and possible storms in the evening. I opened the door and heard the rumble of thunder in the distance. I have always enjoyed hearing turkeys gobble at thunder so I thought I would go ahead and go hunting. However, as I began getting ready, I heard the unmistakable sound of rainfall. While I enjoy hearing turkeys gobble at thunder, I do not enjoy sitting in the rain. Therefore, I decided to go back to bed.

About an hour later I was awakened by my wife, who said the weather was getting bad and she thought I should get up. I went to the door to look out. As I began to open the door, the wind nearly jerked it out of my hand. I noticed the trees were no longer vertical but were bent until they were perpendicular with the ground. I forced the door shut and told my wife to go to the basement.

Fortunately, the storm was short lived. Unfortunately, it doesn't take eighty- to ninety-mile-per-hour straight-line winds long to do significant damage. The middle of the county was devastated with thousands of trees down, numerous homes damaged, and days without electricity. From my porch I could see seventeen trees that were either blown down or had the tops blown out. A later canvas of the remainder of my property revealed a lot of devastation. However, I must tell you that although the storm did millions of dollars' worth of damage to our county, no one was injured during the storm. Praise be to God.

After days of clearing trees from my driveway and having hooked up the generator I decided the next morning I would get back to the woods. Although I knew there were turkeys on the property, my owl hoot did not receive a reply. I wondered if this would be the first day of the season I had not heard a gobble. After several minutes I heard a distant gobble. I immediately placed it as beyond the lower pasture and across the creek on the adjacent property. I had been fortunate enough to call turkeys across the creek in the past and started moving in that direction.

As I moved toward the pasture, through a hole in the trees I spotted two strutting gobblers in the pasture. I knew they were not the turkey I had heard gobble. As I was quickly looking for a tree where I could set up, I noticed movement at the wood line and saw two more strutting gobblers. I hastily sat down. I now had four strutting turkeys within one hundred yards and another gobbling bird in the distance. Once settled in, I could hear the constant drumming emanating from the birds. I gave a low yelp and gobbler number six gobbled behind me. It was obvious this was going to be a monumental day.

Soon a lone hen came through the pasture and the two birds at the wood line immediately followed her while gobbling at my yelping. With them out of sight, I turned my attention to the strutters in the pasture. They eventually moved into the woods with me and strutted and drummed at everything I offered from about fifty-five yards away. Suddenly, my next yelp received a resounding gobble from my left. I watched as two gobblers walked directly to the two strutters I was watching and the strut fest was on. I think these were the two gobblers that were closest to me to start with, but I wasn't sure. If you are thinking you need a score card to keep up with this, you should have been there!

After a long while and probably one hundred gobbles the foursome moved off to the east. I had already decided I needed to move up the ridge toward the birds and quickly made that move. I got set and called and immediately receive several hardy gobbles. Although I could not see them, I judged the birds to be seventy-five yards down the ridge. While listening to the gobbling, I felt something crawling on my right leg. I had already picked up a couple of ticks earlier and thought I probably had another one. However, I soon realized it wasn't a tick and it wasn't an it; it was a them and a lot of them. If you have never hunted in an area with fire ants, you have missed out on a good bit of pain. I looked down to see my right boot covered with ants. With the gobblers seventy-five yards away, I was doing my best to kill the ants with as little movement as possible. I quickly gathered my gear and limped about fifteen yards to another tree and again began killing the biting horde. A glance at my watch revealed I had been engaged with the turkeys for over two hours.

With the majority of the ants subdued, I again called to the birds and received enthusiastic gobbles in return. Soon there were four gobblers making their way to my location. I realized if they stayed on course they were going to walk in front of me at about forty yards. This time the birds were on a pretty steady march and I readied my 20-gauge for a shot. As the lead bird stepped into an opening I did something I had not done in a long time. Something I had warned so many new hunters not to do. I looked to see if I had killed the turkey before I finished making the shot. I fired at the bird and immediately jumped up to go to the bird as I had done so many times before. However, the bird evidently did not know he was supposed to be dead seeing how he turned and quickly walked away followed by two others! A fourth bird got up and flew off to my left. I stood there dumbfounded. I could not believe I had made such a boneheaded mistake. It had been a long time since I had missed a turkey.

I went and looked to be sure there wasn't a bird or any evidence of a hit there. Finding nothing I dejectedly walked back to the tree I had shot from. Just then I heard the unmistakable sound of a turkey fight. Evidently the bird that flew away had flown right into some other gobblers who did not appreciate the intrusion. I stepped out into the field and could actually see three birds fighting in the woods. The birds evidently saw me and began moving away while still beating on each other. I wondered to myself how many times could I mess up in one day. Utterly frustrated, I began walking toward my truck. Just before I reached the truck the fighting turkeys gobbled. Thinking I didn't have much to lose, I went and set up where I had seen the birds fighting minutes earlier.

I got settled in and gave a yelp and a cut. The gobbler over the ridge to the west gobbled and a gobbler back where I had just shot not fifteen minutes earlier gobbled. This was unreal. Within ten minutes I spotted the gobbler to the east at about eighty yards. About the time I saw him, the gobbler above me gobbled. The bird to the east turned and walked into a drain. While he gobbled every time I called, he evidently wasn't looking for a fight.

The gobbler above me gobbled again and I could tell he was closing the distance. Within a few minutes I again heard wing flapping and fighting above me. Then I heard a drum. Although I could not spot the bird I could tell he was close. It's always difficult for me to pinpoint drumming. I made a slight adjustment so I was pointing to where I thought it was coming from. In just a minute I spotted a gobbler crossing the pasture about 125 yards from me. I did not know if it was the gobbler that had just been above me or yet another bird. Soon I received the answer to that question when I spotted a fan on the ridge above me. The gobbler was about fifty yards from me. Suddenly a second gobbler popped up beside him and they both began easing my way. Unbelievably a third gobbler emerged from behind them. Closer inspection revealed the third bird was a jake. I was pretty worked up but I guess since I had already been through so much I was not close to hyperventilating as I usually am! However, that was about to change when gobbler number two started quickly closing the distance between us while my gun was pointed toward gobbler number one.

Now I had gobbler two at twenty-five yards and looking for me and gobbler one and the jake at thirty-five yards and obscured by trees. I thought to myself that I sure needed something to happen and it did. Evidently the jake got just a little too close to gobbler one and he ran at him. That separated the birds and placed gobbler number one directly in front of my front bead. Remembering to keep my head down, I shot the bird at thirty-two steps. Gobbler number two began putting and he and the jake ran back over the ridge. I moved over and admired my double-bearded trophy. I knelt down over the bird and thanked the Lord above for the most eventful hunt of my career. As I looked at the five- and ten-inch beards and one-and-a-quarter-inch spurs, the gobbler over the ridge gobbled.

At least six adult gobblers seen, at least seven gobblers heard gobbling 202 times, and fifteen fire ant bites in a three-hour-and-forty-five-minute marathon hunt in the middle of a pandemic. Yep, that's a season like no other I had ever experienced.

In my pandemic season the numbers were unbelievable. Obviously, many of these turkeys were the same birds. I heard seventy-two gobblers gobble 2,335 times. Yes, I count every gobble!

One day heard eight gobblers, 173 gobbles.

One day heard seven gobblers, 202 gobbles.

One day heard five gobblers, 266 gobbles.

One day heard three gobblers, 423 gobbles.

One day heard five gobblers, 300-plus gobbles.

Many days it was one or two birds.

My God is an awesome God and I thank Him for creation and letting me enjoy it!

Recycling Turkeys

THE OLD GOBBLER HAD BEEN PURSUED hard for the past couple of years. Living on property leased to a hunting club, the bird had become a master of survival. He had heard every type of call and had likely had several close encounters. Although he was within one hundred yards of the highway, he had walked across this hill many times. It was as if he knew he was out of range of the many turkey hunters who had pursued him. This winter he was simply trying to find enough food to make it until things began to green up in the spring. Unfortunately, he did not realize everyone didn't play by the rules. He didn't think much about the truck stopped in the road until he felt the 30-06 bullet tear through his breast and then heard the shot that ended his existence. Or did it?

Luckily, the club president heard the shot from the clubhouse and immediately called and reported the incident. I arrived on the scene a few minutes later. The president relayed the story to me. When he told me he had observed one individual on the ground and a green "game warden" Bronco passing the location, I knew the vehicle was in fact an old game warden truck that now belonged to a veteran outlaw locally known as Big Slimy.

Since it was deer season, I immediately assumed Big Slimy had shot a deer. The hunting club had been on the Deer Management Assistance Program for several years and had many good bucks on the property. I called Conservation Enforcement

Officer (CEO) Shannon Calfee and asked him to come to my location. He soon arrived and I explained what had occurred. We speculated that having an individual "on the ground" indicated an attempt to retrieve whatever had been shot. After a few minutes of searching, Shannon called me and said he had located it. I asked if it was a buck and he replied, "No, it's a turkey." I must admit it had not crossed my mind we might be looking for a turkey; however, now we had one.

I would much rather we had found a dead deer on the side of that mountain. Anyone who will kill a turkey illegally is the lowest of the low in my book. They most definitely shouldn't be allowed to call themselves a turkey hunter. This resentment is likely rooted in the many thrilling mornings the wild turkey has provided for me. It is difficult to put into words the feeling I have when a gobbler's drumming sounds like it is coming from every side and I'm holding my breath and scanning the landscape with eyes looking for that baseball riding a shadow that is in actuality the gobbler's head. Just writing those words, I get a little excited thinking about the next time it will happen. To think some criminal would steal that moment from legitimate hunters turns my stomach.

I think if asked, many seasoned turkey hunters would have to admit feeling at least a tinge of remorse after harvesting a gobbler. The fact the bird supplied such a thrilling experience leads me to wish there were some way to bring him back to life. As a certified wildlife biologist, I very well understand you cannot stockpile wildlife. I appreciate the fact the licensed hunter is a vital tool in an effort to keep wildlife populations within the carrying capacity of the habitat. After thirty-six years of pursuing gobblers, I have learned to appreciate the hunt as much as the harvest. Don't misunderstand me, I still nearly hyperventilate when a gobbler gets in close and I still enjoy carrying one out of the woods. However, I would love to have a way to bring gobblers back to life. To recycle them. Believe it or not, I found a way to do just that, almost.

Before you begin to think I have blown a little too hard on my owl hooter, allow me to explain. The turkey illegally killed in the story outlined earlier, was the first turkey I was able to recycle. To say I recycled it is a bit of a misnomer. Actually, my friend, mentor, and former coworker, retired Conservation Enforcement Officer Byron Smith, took the bird and transformed it into a turkey decoy. Not to be used to lure in gobblers, but to catch turkey poachers!

Byron was the owner of Conservation Decoy Company in Wetumpka, Alabama. In his shop, he took animal hides, electronics, and his many years of poacher catching know-how and produced decoys that have no doubt saved the lives of countless wild animals. Although he has created everything from groundhogs to bear decoys, Byron primarily built deer and turkey decoys and worked exclusively with wildlife agencies. These decoys are currently being used across the country to aid conservation law enforcement in their effort to curtail illegal hunting activity.

Officers across the nation have reported these faux toms have been instrumental in numerous arrests of those who fashion themselves as hunters but, in reality, are mere outlaws. Although not necessarily the first to have the decoy idea, Byron has definitely perfected the art of decoy development and use.

Working as a CEO, Byron realized early on that having the violator, officer, and wildlife at the same place at the same time was often difficult. Every officer in areas of prevalent illegal hunting has experienced the frustration of hearing distant shots or having a violator roll slowly by a field without any wildlife present. The creation of the deer decoy drastically changed the way CEOs worked hunting at night and hunting from the road. The decoy allows the officer to dictate to a great extent where a stop will occur, which makes for a much safer situation. The decoy is a great tool for the officer and has facilitated thousands of arrests throughout the country.

Although wild turkeys are intuitively wary, grasses and legumes found growing on roadsides and right-of-ways often lure them. To a turkey, a seldom-traveled road is merely an opening in the woods. Lovesick gobblers are often seen strutting in and along rural roads. Unfortunately, there appears to be no shortage of unscrupulous individuals that will take advantage of this situation. Many so-called hunters who evidently don't possess the skills necessary to a take a wild turkey legally will stoop to shooting one out the window with both shotguns and rifles. Fortunately, the turkey decoy gives the officer the opportunity to be in the same location as the turkey and the violator.

Having supplied numerous decoys to states across the country, Byron regularly receives reports from officers touting the success of the birds. If there is anything I like more than turkey hunting, it's catching someone illegally hunting turkeys. Donating turkey skins to assist other officers in catching violators gives me a great sense of satisfaction.

As a CEO, certified wildlife biologist, and avid turkey hunter, I wholeheartedly supported Byron in his work by skinning the turkeys I killed and allowing him to use them to create decoys. It is very difficult to estimate how much wildlife has been saved by the use of decoys. I cannot tell you how many times I've had someone tell me they have seen my deer decoy. They normally say it didn't look real. However, I don't tell them I'm surprised it didn't look real since it must have been seeing how my decoy was nowhere close to where they reported it! For all you know the last gobbler you killed may have been spared because a poacher knew decoys were in use.

After a thorough investigation, CEO Shannon Calfee and I were able to apprehend the individuals who killed the turkey I mentioned at the beginning of this story. He and his accomplice were both convicted and paid hefty fines. The turkey was recycled and is now used to catch other violators. I can't think of a more fitting way to use a monarch of the woods whose life was cut short.

Carbon Copy Days

As I was talking with my fifteen-year-old turkey hunting partner, I was explaining how difficult it was to hunt turkeys because of their lack of predictableness. I told him that one day they might gobble their heads nearly off and the next day could be a carbon copy and they would not say a word. The look on his face quickly told me he wasn't following what I was saying.

In going back over what I said, I realized it was likely the carbon copy comment that had thrown him off. Obviously, a fifteen-year-old has no idea what carbon paper is. Therefore, I took a moment to explain that carbon paper was used to make a copy prior to everyone having copy machines in their office. I explained when you placed the sheet of carbon paper between two pieces pf paper and wrote on the top sheet everything would show up on the second sheet. It was obvious he had never heard of such a thing. I remembered again, I'm old as dirt!

How is it that turkeys decide that today is the day they will gobble? If I knew the answer to that, I'm sure I would be on a nationwide lecture circuit! I have heard several theories put forth but nothing that has been proven. My dear friend Phillip Blake, who was seated right beside me on my first ever turkey kill many years ago, told me something that day that I have found to be so true. He said a turkey is a fickle bird and it does what it wants to do when it wants to do it! If you look up the definition of *fickle* it says "changing frequently." *Capricious* is listed as a synonym and is defined as "given to sudden and unaccountable changes of behavior." There was not a picture of a gobbler in the dictionary, but I think there should be!

Just this week I hunted the same spot three days in a row. The first day I had two gobblers in a clear-cut in front of me and had a third gobbler, that never gobbled only drummed, come up behind me. I counted eighty-two gobbles. The second day was much the same; however, the non-gobbling bird was now gobbling before daylight and the other two were silent. Once the previously non-gobbler flew down, he never said another word but the other two begin gobbling. I recorded sixty-two gobbles. Day three, which was another carbon copy day, I heard one turkey and it gobbled one time. Hey they're fickle birds!

When I became the area manager for the Coosa Wildlife Management Area (WMA) I quickly learned the WMA was a turkey hunting hot spot. The area drew hunters from across the country as well as many locals. A fellow I met early on was Ole Billy Connelley. That was the way Billy would identify himself anytime he ever called me. Billy and his wife, Mae, and later their sons all hunted the WMA. They were good hunters and enjoyed a lot of success. I have always remembered a conversation I had with Billy one morning. I was set up checking turkey hunters as they left the area. Billy pulled up and had a fine gobbler. He told me this was the sixth day he had hunted the same location. He said he had located good turkey sign in the area but had not heard a turkey gobbler for the past five days. This morning he had heard five turkeys gobbling like rip. We neither one could explain what had changed to cause the birds to sound off. I surely don't know how to explain this phenomenon; however, it could be the reason I go back every day! I think Phil nailed it. They're fickle birds!

If you're going to hunt turkeys, you will need to learn the turkey hunting vernacular! If you don't know what a carbon copy day is, ask someone over forty years old!

New Mexico

ONE OF THE HIGHLIGHTS of my career as a wildlife biologist was my opportunity to work with the 4-H Wildlife Habitat Evaluation Program. It was my good fortune to coach several teams and to be asked to serve on the national committee that administrated the contest. I signed on for a three-year term and stayed for fourteen years!

One of the many enjoyable parts of being on the committee was the opportunity to travel across the country and see many beautiful places. Each year the contest was held in a different state. The normal routine was for some of the committee members to travel to the selected state in the spring to view the site and make sure everything would be in place for the contest, which was normally held in July.

It just so happened that the year the contest was to be held in New Mexico, the spring trip coincided with turkey season. The extension wildlife specialist at the time was Dr. Jon Boren. Jon extended an invitation for a turkey hunt while I was there. Obviously, he did not realize I was addicted to turkey hunting. I quickly accepted the offer.

I was very excited to hunt turkeys in New Mexico. John had told me we would be hunting in the Gila National Forest, where he was currently conducting elk research. The chance to possibly see some elk in the wild excited me that much more.

At this time, I had only hunted outside of my home state of Alabama once or twice and those hunts had been in Texas. Preparing for the trip, I assumed the climate in New Mexico would probably be pretty much like Texas and therefore packed accordingly.

This would be the first time I had flown with a firearm so I read up on what was required. I purchased a hard case. When I arrived at the Birmingham airport I told the lady at the counter I had a firearm to declare. She told me she would have someone come and check it. In just a minute a fellow showed up. He asked if the gun was unloaded and I told him it was. He viewed it and dropped a tag in the case and told me to close it up and give it to the attendant at the desk. Smooth sailing.

We arrived in New Mexico and checked out everything for the contest. There were several aspects to laying out a contest. Any time you were bringing a hundred kids, parents, and coaches to a site you didn't want any hiccups.

With everything related to the contest checked out, it was time to get to the hunt. So far, I had been right about the climate; however, I was about to learn some interesting information. I was told by Jon that we would be staying in a small town called Cloudcroft and we would be hunting on the mountain above the town. That sounded fine to me. Not having many mountains in central Alabama, I didn't see any problems.

I had carried my normal turkey hunting apparel, which consisted of a camouflage T-shirt and a pair of camouflage overalls. Just in case, I had thrown in a light camo jacket. We arrived in the late afternoon at Cloudcroft. We made plans to leave early the next morning. I was told it would take about thirty minutes to get to our hunting area.

I had trouble sleeping; however, I must have slept some seeing how I heard some complaints about someone snoring.

Since I didn't hear it, I figured I must have slept through it! It was a mild sixty-two degrees and I was raring to go. We loaded up and headed out. Or maybe I should say headed up. Almost immediately we were headed up hill and we continued to climb for the next thirty minutes. I quickly began to realize I had been remiss in not having paid more attention to the area I would be hunting. If I had, I might have learned that it was at nine thousand feet of elevation! I could tell in the vehicle that the temperature seemed to be dropping a little bit. When we reached our hunting area, it was thirty-seven degrees with a steady wind. Thank goodness I had grabbed my light jacket. Not hearing any turkeys gobble made for a *cold* morning. However, it was a beautiful day and I did receive a thrill. As I sat on the edge of an opening, calling occasionally, I heard a limb break off to my right. I slowly turned my head in time to see an elk step out into the opening. It was beautiful and so were the next thirty-five that stepped out! It was quite a day.

No one had heard any turkeys. Fortunately, we had another day. However, when we arrived back in Cloudcroft we found Jon waiting on us. He asked how things had gone and I told him it had gone fine and I didn't think I was going to lose any toes due to frostbite! He then told me he had a request for me. He explained the dean of New Mexico State University had approached him wanting to go on a turkey hunt and since Jon didn't hunt, he wanted to know if I would take him the next morning. I told him I would be happy to take him; however, based on how well I had done today, I hope he didn't expect too much. He told me Dean Chicken Dance would be there the next morning. I could honestly say that I had never heard of anyone named what I understood as Chicken Dance and I felt certain Jon was messing with me. I asked if he could repeat that name and he explained the name was Schickendanz, which was still nothing I had ever heard of.

The next morning the dean and I headed back up the mountain. It was once again quite brisk. I tried to keep moving to keep the blood flowing and generate a little warmth. We had listened at a few spots without hearing any gobbles. I was beginning to wonder whether or not turkeys even responded to owl hoots. Not having hunted much outside of Alabama, I had assumed my turkey hunting tactics would work anywhere. You know what folks say about assuming things! However, I gave another hoot and lo and behold I heard what sounded like a really muffled gobble. I asked the dean if he heard it and said he did. I told him we would try to get a little closer.

One of the things that often presents a challenge when hunting in another state is the terrain and figuring out just how to set up. Trying to hide behind a cow patty in Colorado comes to mind! New Mexico was no exception. In this area the terrain was fairly rugged with a lot of rock. In Alabama, there is normally always a tree to set up against. That definitely wasn't the case in our current location. I kept looking and finally found a small tree on a fairly level spot. I told the dean to sit up against the tree so he could shoot to our left. I hurriedly got set up and removed my aluminum slate from my vest. I looked at the dean and was surprised to see he had set up to where he could shoot straight in front of us but not to the left. I whispered to him the turkey was to our left and he replied he thought it was in front of us. I felt pretty sure I had a good read on where the bird was; however, I told him to listen and I cut at the bird on my mouth call. The bird immediately gobbled. Although the gobbler was again a muffled little effort, I could tell the bird was closer and I could tell for sure the bird was off to our left. I told the dean to turn to his left and he again said the bird was straight in front of him. I really didn't know what to do. The way we were set up the dean was directly between me and where I felt the turkey would show up. I feared neither one of us would end up getting a shot at the bird but the only thing I knew to do was try and call the bird in.

I yelped on my tried-and-true aluminum Thunderdome and there was an immediate gobble. I estimated the bird was probably fifty yards. The dean looked at me and I pointed in the direction of the gobble, which was to his left. The dean turned his head to the left just as the bird strutted into view at about thirty yards. Picture this: the dean's gun was pointed at twelve o'clock, the gobbler was standing in a strut at nine o'clock, and I was at three o'clock. Unfortunately, I had seen this type of set up before and it normally never turned out well. I wasn't exactly sure just what to do. There was no way I could get a shot from my location and I felt certain the bird would not stay put while the dean attempted to get into a shooting position.

What happened next reminded me I definitely wasn't in Alabama anymore. As the turkey looked straight at us with nothing but rocky ground between us, the dean slowly and deliberately began turning his body and his gun toward the gobbler. I knew there was no possible way a wild turkey would stand still long enough for the dean to get into position. I was wondering if there would be any possibility to call this bird back after the movement spooked him. I knew it wouldn't be likely.

The dean continued to turn and adjust. It was like watching a traffic accident happening. I could see it coming but there wasn't anything I could do about it. As I waited for the bird to exit, I could not believe it when the bird never moved. As I watched in shock, the dean got his gun to his shoulder and lined up his sights on the bird. I wanted to scream, *"Shoot!"* However, I thought this was working so far so I had better let it play out. What seemed like a minute was probably about ten seconds. I couldn't hold it any longer and I whispered to the dean to shoot. Finally, the dean pulled the trigger and the gobbler hit the ground flopping.

I ran to the bird and made sure he was dead. The entire time I was thinking there was no way this would have happened in Alabama. I grabbed the bird and brought it back to where the dean was still seated. He was excited and I was amazed! I swear I have had turkeys spot me when I have not moved a muscle much less turned my whole body around. I've had turkeys see and hear me take my safety off at forty yards and hit the wind. While I know I'm biased, I will always believe if you can consistently kill mature gobblers in Alabama, you can kill one anywhere!

Jon was delighted to learn the dean had harvested a bird. He dubbed me the turkey hunting guru. I assured him I was no turkey hunting guru and we were very fortunate to have been able to close the deal on this fine bird. I have remembered this hunt many times, often when I have made the slightest move and an Alabama gobbler has hit the wind!

It was now time to gather everything up and head to the airport in El Paso. Once again, I "assumed" things would basically function the same way when I went to board the plane. Once again, I was about to be reminded I wasn't in Alabama anymore. Just as I had done in Birmingham, I went to the counter and told the attendant I had a firearm to declare. She immediately turned around and yelled, "He's got a gun!" She did not say this to someone standing nearby or to another attendant, she just screamed it! I immediately started looking to see which direction the shots were going to come from. To my relief, there was no immediate reaction. Eventually someone came walking up and opened my case and looked at the gun and handed me a card to fill out and place inside. The rest of the trip was uneventful.

Fortunately, on another hunt on some flat ground in New Mexico I was able to take a Merriam's. That's another good story. You may see it later!

If He Hadn't
Stepped on My Foot!

I FEEL IT IS SAFE TO SAY the better you know a property, the more successful you will be when hunting it. Take it from me, the turkeys know the property! Knowing the layout will help in deciding where and how to set up on a bird. Of course, you can't forget that some turkeys are magicians!

I was hunting a friend's property one morning and had chased a faraway gobble only to have the bird shut up before I could really get close. As I eased back toward the truck, I heard a gobble in front of me. I quickly figured out the bird was in a wildlife opening about a hundred yards ahead of me. I got as close as I dared and sat down and yelped to the bird.

I was setting on the side of a woods road about seventy-five yards from the opening where I felt sure the gobbler was standing. Of course, you always have to keep in mind that the bird may be moving at the same time you are.

I gave another yelp, which was immediately answered by a gobble by the bird that was *not* standing seventy yards in front of me but was forty yards to my right. I must admit it startled me just a bit. Unfortunately, there was nothing between me and the turkey but air so moving was not an option.

Amazingly the bird began walking straight to me at a quick pace. I could feel myself starting to hyperventilate a little bit. Within thirty seconds the gobbler was standing about eight steps to my right! Keep in mind it is not a good idea to move when a turkey is moving right toward you. Although I did not have my gun to my shoulder, I did not move. The gun was across my knee with the stock in my right hand by my side. The bird began walking again and I realized it was going to walk directly in front of me at a distance of about ten feet! I could not believe this was happening.

As the bird slowly walked in front of me I maneuvered my gun so the bead of my gun was on his head. I did not think about the fact the stock was down by my side. When the bead got on the bird's head, I pulled the trigger. I'm sure the shot went feet above the turkey's head. He hit the wind and I tried to stop hyperventilating. I've always said I would have killed him if he hadn't stepped on my foot! One of the best parts of turkey hunting was you never knew what a turkey might do. This one got away but I feel certain he probably spent some time wondering just what had happened! It's amazing how well they can see and they will still step into your lap! Not knowing what might happen is one of the things that keeps me going. I hope I get a chance to go back!

Last Hunt

WHILE MY DADDY wasn't an avid hunter, he realized I wanted to be and bless his heart he set out to help me. The way he did that was by setting me up with three guys who he knew were avid hunters and whom he trusted to teach me how to hunt. The three guys' names were Don, Freddie, and Jerry. They were addicted to deer hunting and set out to addict me as well. We primarily hunted on the Lauderdale Wildlife Management Area in Waterloo, Alabama. The area was often crowded, which brought on numerous situations.

These guys did a pretty good job of teaching me basic hunting techniques and safety. I very much appreciated their efforts. There was one thing that stood out the most during my tutelage. I have repeated it to others hundreds of times. After observing something quite unusual, Jerry told me this. He said if you spend a lot of time in the woods, you are going to see things that people will not believe. He then said, "And it's usually best just not to tell them about it!" I have found that to be so true. I've seen a lot of things that I have just kept to myself rather than endure the scorn.

During my last turkey season, I once again made a couple of interesting observations. I and my sixteen-year-old hunting companion were sitting in my truck waiting for the sky to lighten a little when he asked me if there were any cell towers on the property we were hunting on. Of course, only a few years earlier there were no cell towers in our small rural county. However, things change and we had finally moved into the twenty-first century and come up with a tower or two. However, there were no towers on the property we were now on and I told him so.

Of course, his next question was, "What's that light?" as he pointed out the front windshield. I looked out in front of the truck maybe thirty yards and there at about fifteen feet above the ground was a bright white light about the size of a cell phone. The light was on, then it went off, very much like a lightning bug. As we watched the light would go on and off in lightning bug fashion. It made no sound as it moved from right to left. It illuminated probably five or six times as it moved to our left, never making a sound. I never saw it again although I hunted there many days. Go figure.

Only a couple of days later, I'm back in the same spot waiting on daylight. I've gotten out of the truck and heard an unsolicited gobble from No Kill Ridge. For the past thirty years it has been the rare feat to take a bird from the sharp ridge that gives them all the advantages. I've learned that there is a much better chance of success if I don't try to get on this ridge with the birds but rather try to coax them off of it, which was my quick plan.

I quickly dropped off into a drain that leads me around to the hayfield where I should at least be able to see the gobblers even if I can't get them in close enough. The birds continue to gobble as I work around and I decide there are four gobblers on the ridge. I am in place approximately 125 yards from the birds when I hear the first one fly down. Within a minute there are four mature gobblers out in front of me. The birds are strutting and carrying on. I've not heard or seen a hen. The birds are doing what I love to watch them do on a beautiful crisp morning. I love watching them carry on and I'm not worried about trying to take one of them. I'm wishing I had my young hunter or my son with me. I've taken plenty of turkeys and would much rather see them get a bird. I'm very content watching the birds, which are about seventy yards in front of me.

As I watch, the four gobblers are all in a strut in front of me when I have a first-time event occur. One of the mature gobblers proceeds to sit down in the field in full strut. He simply squats to the ground and just sits there looking around. The three others are in full strut and parading around as usual, while this bird just sits there watching. He isn't gyrating on the ground or anything, he is just sitting there looking around. I had never seen this type of behavior before.

Eventually, the bird stood up, having never coming out of his strut. He strutted a few feet and once again sat down in full strut. He eventually did this four times. He then stood up, came out of strut, and just walked across the field into the woods where I was set up. Once again, my mind was running wide open as to what this was all about. As I watched, the bird walked past me at about thirty-five yards. I raised my gun and placed my sight on his neck and watched as he walked past. Why I didn't shoot him I'm not really sure, but it likely has to do with him putting on a show unlike any I had ever seen! While I still enjoy taking a turkey from time to time, I learned a long time ago that it's about the show. I have been so richly blessed.

Now, with a terminal cancer diagnosis, I prepare to head toward my home in heaven. I am anxious to see what awaits. I'm not sure whether or not I'll be able to sit and talk with turkeys or if we will keep up our cat-and-mouse games. Either way, I know as I leave here, I have been richly blessed. And just maybe before long I'll have a few things I've seen that it was best not to tell people about explained in full. We shall see. Thanks for listening. Choose eternal life, choose Jesus. God bless.

Epilogue

AS I'M SURE YOU CAN GUESS, this collection just touched the surface of thirty-six years of turkey hunting. Unfortunately, my opportunity to get more stories written was cut short by melanoma cancer. Although no one in my family had ever had cancer, I was diagnosed with it last year and despite treatment it has progressively gotten worse. As a matter of fact, I did not think I would finish this book but the good Lord allowed me to do so.

One of my favorite things about turkey hunting was being out there at daylight and hearing creation come to life. I can't understand how anyone can experience that and believe there isn't a God above. How someone can experience a gobbler putting on his show and think that was not created by a superior being is beyond me. As you read in many of these stories, I always knelt over every gobbler and thanked the Lord for creating nature and allowing me to experience it. I'm not sure what heaven is like but I understand it will be better than earth. I'm not sure I'm going to be able to stand it!

I'm going to find out soon. You may be headed to eternity quicker than you think. Now is the time to choose the Lord as your savior. I hope you enjoy these stories and they inspire you to get out and engage the wild turkey. About the time you think you have him figured out, he will teach you something new.

I want to once again thank my turkey hunting mentors for their efforts to introduce me to the monarch of the woods. It was a large part of my life that I truly enjoyed.

God bless.

One Final Note

Joel was correct in his assumption that he wouldn't make it through the publishing of his last three books. I promised him that I would see that they were finished. With the publishing of this final book, I have kept my promise.

In October of 2023, we were given the terrible news that the melanoma had metastasized to Joel's central nervous system. We were told that he had a matter of weeks to months. He was able to stay with us an additional six months and five days.

Nine days prior to his homegoing, his dear friend and longtime hunting partner Blake was able to take him on one last successful turkey hunt. It was a beautiful day for all of us.

On April 6, 2024, he passed away peacefully while I was sitting next to him and quietly holding his hand. We were surrounded by loved ones. I miss him every day.

Melanie

Joel and Blake (pictured with Joel's faithful companion Brownie) on their last hunt together after thirty-six years as hunting partners and shared incidents that spawned innumerable stories and much laughter.

Our family chose to honor Joel by using the turkey feathers, fan, beard, and feet with spurs from his final turkey hunt in the spray of flowers for his funeral service. It was very fitting and a perfect tribute to his love of the wild turkey.